# the **diabetes**
## menu cookbook

# the **diabetes** menu cookbook

Delicious Special-Occasion Recipes
for Family and Friends

BARBARA SCOTT-GOODMAN

AND

KALIA DONER, EDITOR IN CHIEF OF DIABETES FOCUS

PHOTOGRAPHS BY JUDD PILOSSOF

Nutritional Advisors

Christine Gerbstadt, M.D., M.P.H.
Certified Diabetes Educator (CDE), Registered Dietician,
National Spokesperson, American Dietetic Association

Virginia Zamudio, R.N., CDE,
former president of the American Association of Diabetes Educators

JOHN WILEY & SONS, INC.

This book is printed on acid-free paper. ⊗

Published by John Wiley & Sons, Inc., Hoboken, New Jersey
Published simultaneously in Canada

Book Design: Barbara Scott-Goodman
Food Stylists: William Smith, Liz Duffy
Prop Stylists: Phyllis Asher, Randi Barritt

The authors would also like to thank Janet Scott for additional recipe testing
and Christopher Hampton for additional nutritional research.

For general information about our other products and services, please contact our
Customer Care Department within the United States at (800) 762-2974,
outside the United States at (317) 572-3993 or fax (317) 572-4002.

Wiley also publishes its books in a variety of electronic formats.
Some content that appears in print may not be available in electronic books.
For more information about Wiley products, visit our web site at www.wiley.com.

*Library of Congress Cataloging-in-Publication Data:*
Scott-Goodman, Barbara.
The diabetes menu cookbook : delicious special-occasion recipes for family and friends
Barbara Scott-Goodman and Kalia Doner ;
diabetes focus nutritional advisors Christine Gerbstadt, Virginia Zamudio.
    p. cm.
ISBN-10: 0-471-78246-7 (cloth)
ISBN-13: 978-0-471-78246-9 (cloth)
1. Diabetes--Diet therapy--Recipes. I. Scott-Goodman, Barbara. II. Title.
RC662.S39 2006
641.5'6314--dc22

                                        2006001932

Printed in the United States of America

10  9  8  7  6  5  4  3  2  1

# contents

# foreword

Almost 21 million Americans, or 7 percent of the population, have diabetes. More than 90 percent of these people have type 2—what doctors used to call adult onset. But recent changes have made the term inaccurate: Type 2 diabetes now occurs in young children as well as in adults. And the number of people who suffer from it is increasingly rapidly.

The goal for people with diabetes is to achieve normal blood glucose through diet, medication, and exercise—and, as a consequence, reduce the complications associated with the disease, such as heart and kidney disease.

Accomplishing this task may seem monumental at first. But there are steps to take that can make a big difference. First, put together a good team of health advisors including a registered dietitian who can help design a meal plan that suits your lifestyle and food preferences. Then put your meal plan into action.

That's where resources such as *The Diabetes Menu Cookbook* come in handy! Many people newly diagnosed with diabetes worry that they may never again eat the foods they love. This becomes especially tough at holidays and at parties. But it is simply not true! Now you can enjoy your favorite foods while achieving control of your diabetes.

*The Diabetes Menu Cookbook* provides sample menus and easy-to-follow recipes so you can enjoy a healthy diet that tastes fantastic. You may even feel like you are cheating on your diet because the foods taste so delicious, but don't worry, all of these recipes can fit into your meal plan. And, in fact, anyone striving to eat a healthy diet can enjoy every single recipe and menu plan in this book.

And while *The Diabetes Menu Cookbook* gives you the basic information you need to count carbohydrates, use exchanges and calculate total calories, fat grams, or saturated fat, it also takes healthy, diabetes-friendly cuisine to the next level of sophistication. *The Diabetes Menu Cookbook* gives you a plan for celebrating your life deliciously!

*Christine Gerbstadt, M.D., M.P.H., R.D.*
National Spokesperson American Dietetic Association

# celebrate your life!

We've got a secret, and we are willing to tell it to anyone who wants in on it. Great festive, fabulous food, and smart diabetes management are not enemies! One of the best kept secrets in America is that great food and good times can be good for you.

As editor of *Diabetes Focus,* I am lucky to have gotten to know hundreds of readers who, like you, are trying to find a way to combine a new approach to eating with a love of food and a zest for throwing a party. I will never forget Elsie, who wrote to tell me about her first Thanksgiving dinner after she was diagnosed with type 2 diabetes. "I was sure I would either have to starve myself—passing up my favorite holiday flavors like stuffing and gravy—so my guests could enjoy the meal, or serve them cardboard and cranberry sauce! I've always been the one to host this family get-together—and I didn't want to give it up. Your magazine's recipes from Barbara Scott-Goodman offered great holiday dinner ideas. No one noticed that I had designed the meal so that it was low in fat, filled with tasty vegetables and whole grains, and offered a choice of desserts that the most weight conscious person could enjoy. I tested myself before I ate, took my medication, and then tested after the meal. My glucose level wasn't perfect, but considering what I had been expecting, it was a real blessing. Thank you!"

Over the past several years, Barbara and I have learned so much from people like Elsie who have faced the challenges of changing their eating habits and learned new ways to take charge of their health without losing the pleasure they get from cooking and celebrating.

Other readers tell stories about how their enjoyment of food has blossomed since they were diagnosed. "I never cooked anything from scratch before I started trying your recipes," wrote one 50-year-old man from Georgia. "I can't believe what I was missing. It's like I am enjoying real food for the first time. In that way I am thankful for my diabetes. It really made my life better." Now he has friends over for summer grill-outs, he's the toast of the neighborhood and 40 pounds thinner, and he reports his last A1c test came in at a healthy 6%.

The input from readers such as these has excited us about the culinary possibilities that diabetes cuisine offers to the serious cook and anyone creating a festive home meal. That's why Barbara and I have joined forces to help you enjoy entertaining and banish your diabetes mealtime blues.

## Let's Get Cooking!

Now it's time to get down to particulars: We are going to help you learn how to prepare a menu that sticks to your new guidelines for nutritional health. Specifically, the new guidelines from the American Diabetes Association recommend that carbohydrate and monounsaturated fat intake should account for 60% to 70% of calorie intake for people with diabetes, and 15% to 20% should come from protein. In addition, the guidelines suggest that less than 10% of caloric intake should come from saturated fats. The American Diabetes Association, American Heart Association, and American Cancer Society, working together, say that you should shoot for:

- Six ounces or less of poultry, fish, or lean meat. (This is a daily allowance, so consider intake at all meals.)

- At least ½ cup to 1 cup of vegetables as part of the meal and a medium-size piece of fruit or ½ cup of fruit salad. Eat a total of at least five servings of fruit and vegetables a day.

- Whole-grain breads and cereals.

- Low-fat soups seasoned with a small amount of salt.

- Healthy fats. Examples include vegetable oils (such as olive, peanut, soybean, and canola oils), avocados, nuts, and trans fat–free, soft, low-fat margarine. You may include these healthy fats in moderate amounts.

- A small-size modest dessert, as an occasional treat. Split large desserts with family or friends.

- A balance of your physical activity and food intake. Try to get 30 minutes of physical activity a day at least 5 days a week.

Overall, each individual's metabolic profile and need to lose weight should determine the total fat intake. But it can be hard to maintain those standards when you are entertaining.

One woman emailed me: "When I think about cooking dinner for my husband's boss next week I think I will faint. I mean, it's scary enough to do a meal like that without this pressure to stick with food that's on my nutritional plan. Would it be rude to eat my own dinner first and then just eat a salad when they are here? It's enough to make me go live in a cave!"

Bad idea. Get into the spotlight! You can shine, even in such potentially difficult situations. And you deserve it. Nothing provides us with a sense of connection, affection, and relaxation like a good party or get-together. Unfortunately, these occasions are loaded with "ought tos" and "shoulds."

We expect to serve rich, indulgent food at a dinner party; to imbibe a bit too much at a wedding celebration; or wade into luscious desserts at a birthday party. We may want to pay closer attention to our diets, but it is hard. Well, this book offers alternatives and solutions, so that when you are the host you can set out a great tasting feast that satisfies everyone and still provides you with a healthy selection of good eats.

Let's cut to the chase. There are five simple rules to follow when it comes to putting together a party menu that is good for you and wows your guests.

1. Saturated fat is the lazy cook's shortcut to flavor. You do not need it to make a tasty feast.
2. Fiber-rich carbohydrates (whole grains, green vegetables) satisfy your craving for carbs without loading you up with glucose-zonking foods.
3. Simple food is not boring food, if it is made with the best ingredients, pure, fresh, and packed with flavor and texture. As Barbara says, "All great dishes begin with great ingredients. They are nurtured through the preparation, cutting, and combining. The least of it all is the actual cooking!"
4. When entertaining, your meal is your gift to your guests. Always put it in a pretty package and they will feel like they are special. In other words, take some time with presentation, and no one will miss the calorie bombs you may have once delivered.
5. Cook what you like to eat. That's the surest way to infuse the food with love, the best flavor of all.

## Getting Started

Are you ready to take your cooking to the next level?

The first step is to work with your nutritionist, diabetes educator, and physician. Develop a basic plan that outlines your daily dietary goals and your long-range goals for weight management and glucose control. If you do not have a plan, take the time to talk with your diabetes care team about creating one that is tailored to suit your lifestyle—your work schedule, your family habits, and your tastes in food. Then, taking that as a guide, you can look at the various recipes in this book and see what their nutritional analysis offers and how well it fits in with your needs. You will be surprised by how many flavors and foods are available to you that are low in fat and unrefined carbohydrates and sugars. So let's get cooking.

### Making Menu Magic

Integrated throughout the book are menus that bring together the recipes needed to create a complete festive feast. While they are designed to offer you guidance, you should also be fearless about adapting them to any occasion and to combining various recipes to create your own menus.

### Choosing a Menu

A couple of weeks before your dinner party, sit down with this cookbook and plan out what you would like to serve your guests. Use any one of the menus we have included in the book, or mix and match some of the recipes and adapt them to your individual taste. You may decide on a menu based on one special main course, such as chili, a crown roast, or leg of lamb. You may have a type of ethnic food in mind—Tex-Mex, Italian, or Asian. Or there may be a special occasion to celebrate, a holiday, birthday, or anniversary.

**Step 1.** Think in terms of what kind of food the occasion calls for. Casual? Exotic? Kid friendly? Finger food? Comfort food? Formal?

**Step 2.** Make sure you can find the best and freshest ingredients for preparing the dishes you have decided to serve. If some are not readily available—they are out of season or too exotic for your neighborhood grocery store—revise the menu.

**Step 3.** Imagine how the various dishes and course will go together. The basic components of menu construction are taste, texture, balance, and color. You want to provide a variety of textures, colors, and taste, but be sure to maintain a balance that allows them all to harmonize.

## Developing Your Own Style

When it comes to throwing a party or putting together a simple backyard picnic, knowing your strengths and emphasizing your personal style will help you develop new and healthier ways to cook for family, friends, and for all occasions.

Bringing people together for a meal is about giving a gift to your guests— a gift that comes from your heart, expresses your style, and shares comfort and joy. It is not about making yourself into someone you are not, or putting on a show. The sooner you get comfortable with your natural style, the easier it will be to prepare and share party food that respects the health needs of those with diabetes without losing a bit of festive, tasty enjoyment.

# chapter one appetizers

W hen it comes to serving party food, you want to make sure the first bite is the best. Appetizers convey the taste and style of a get-together and let people know you are going all out to make sure they have a great time. The trick is to offer a bounty of flavors, so your guests feel satiated without overeating. At a cocktail party you want the tidbits to seem ample and filling; before a meal you want them to set the stage, not over-whelm all that is to follow. The recipes in this section include salsas and dips—from Black Bean Salsa to Herbed Yogurt & Horseradish Dip—that are as beautiful to the eye as they are to taste. And the heartier Lemon-Rosemary Chicken Bites and so-piquant Pickled Party Shrimp can hold their own with a hungry crowd.

# toasted party nuts

A bowl of almonds and pecans baked with pan-toasted spices is always a welcome treat for a cocktail party spread or for an impromptu snack when friends drop by.

**MAKES 2 CUPS**

½ TEASPOON GROUND CUMIN
½ TEASPOON CHILI POWDER
½ TEASPOON GARLIC SALT
½ TEASPOON GROUND GINGER
½ TEASPOON GROUND CINNAMON
PINCH OF CAYENNE PEPPER
1 TABLESPOON OLIVE OIL
1 CUP ALMONDS
1 CUP PECANS
KOSHER SALT

1.  Preheat the oven to 325°F.
2.  In a small bowl, mix the spices together. Heat the oil in a small skillet over medium heat. Add the spice mixture and cook to blend, stirring constantly, about 3 minutes.
3.  Put the nuts in a large mixing bowl, add the spice mixture and toss well to coat. Spread the nuts on a baking sheet and bake until toasted, 12 to 15 minutes, shaking the pan occasionally. Remove the nuts from the oven, sprinkle with salt to taste and let cool for at least 1 hour.

• *Nutritional content per serving: 6 servings per recipe: Cals.: 247; % of cals. from fat: 89; Fat: 25g; Sat. fat: 2g; Carbs: 6g; Fiber: 4g; Sugars: 1.5g; Cholesterol: 0g; Protein: 5g; Sodium: 301mg*

**NUTS TO YOU !**

Researchers from the Harvard School of Public Health have found that women who eat nuts or peanut butter five times a week or more, significantly lowered the risk for type 2 diabetes compared to women who never or rarely eat nuts or peanut butter. Sprinkling a few nuts on a salad is an easy way to eat more of their heart-healthy unsaturated fats. But be careful! Nuts and oils are high in calories, like all fats. So cut out calories by reducing your intake of other foods to make room for the added nuts in your diet.

# seviche with avocados & tomatoes

Seviche, served with Oven-Baked Pita Crisps (page 18) or Handmade Spicy Tortilla Chips (page 12), is a light and wonderful hors d'oeuvre. This cooling dish, which comes from the hot climes of Latin America, is very easy to prepare. Simply let fresh scallops "cook" for a few hours in a citrus bath of lemons and limes in the refrigerator.

**SERVES 12**

1 POUND BAY SCALLOPS OR SEA SCALLOPS, HALVED
½ CUP FRESH LIME JUICE (ABOUT 4 LIMES)
2 TABLESPOONS FRESH LEMON JUICE (ABOUT ½ LEMON)
½ RED BELL PEPPER, STEMMED, SEEDED, DEVEINED, AND DICED
½ YELLOW BELL PEPPER, STEMMED, SEEDED, DEVEINED, AND DICED
1 JALAPEÑO PEPPER, SEEDED AND FINELY DICED
3 SCALLIONS, TRIMMED AND MINCED (WHITE AND LIGHT GREEN PARTS)
3 TABLESPOONS CHOPPED FRESH CILANTRO
2 TABLESPOONS EXTRA-VIRGIN OLIVE OIL
KOSHER SALT AND FRESHLY GROUND BLACK PEPPER
2 AVOCADOS, PEELED AND DICED
2 MEDIUM TOMATOES, DICED
LIME WEDGES, FOR GARNISH

1. Place the scallops in a large glass bowl and pour over the lime and lemon juices. Add the peppers, scallions, and cilantro and toss together. Add 1 tablespoon of the oil and salt and pepper to taste and toss thoroughly to coat. Cover and refrigerate, allowing the scallops to "cook" and the flavors to blend, 2 to 3 hours. Drain the seviche. Return to the refrigerator if not serving immediately.

2. Put avocados and tomatoes in a bowl with the remaining 1 tablespoon of olive oil and toss gently.

3. Put the seviche in a large bowl or on a platter, garnish with lime wedges, and serve with Pita Crisps or Tortilla Chips.

• *Nutritional content per serving: 12 servings per recipe: Cals.: 111; % of cals. from fat: 56; Fat: 7g; Sat. fat: 1g; Carbs: 6g; Fiber: 3g; Sugars: 2g; Cholesterol: 12mg; Protein: 7g; Sodium: 260mg*

# pickled party shrimp

This Southern-inspired appetizer is always a big hit at cocktail parties. It's also excellent to serve before a holiday dinner because it is very light and low in calories. The shrimp can be made well ahead of time since they marinate for a day or two before serving.

**SERVES 12**

1 CUP TARRAGON VINEGAR
½ CUP WATER
6 SLICES FRESH GINGER
2 TABLESPOONS CORIANDER SEEDS
1 TABLESPOON FENNEL SEEDS
1 TABLESPOON MIXED PEPPERCORNS
2½ POUNDS LARGE SHRIMP
1 RED ONION, THINLY SLICED
1 LEMON, THINLY SLICED
¼ CUP SMALL CAPERS, DRAINED
3 GARLIC CLOVES, THINLY SLICED
PINCH OF CAYENNE PEPPER
4 BAY LEAVES
¾ CUP EXTRA-VIRGIN OLIVE OIL
KOSHER SALT AND FRESHLY GROUND BLACK PEPPER

1. In a medium, nonreactive saucepan, combine the vinegar, water, ginger, coriander and fennel seeds, and peppercorns. Bring to a boil over medium-high heat. Lower the heat and simmer for 10 minutes. Set the pickling mixture aside and let cool completely.

2. Bring a large pot of salted water to a boil. Add the shrimp. Remove from the heat and let stand until the shrimp turn pink, about 3 minutes. Drain, rinse, and let cool completely, then shell and devein the shrimp.

3. Place the shrimp in a large glass or ceramic bowl with the onion, lemon slices, capers, garlic, cayenne pepper, and bay leaves and gently toss together. Whisk the olive oil and salt and pepper into the pickling mixture and pour over the shrimp. Cover tightly and refrigerate for at least 24 hours or up to 3 days.

4. To serve the shrimp, remove them with a slotted spoon, transfer to a platter, and serve cold or at room temperature with toothpicks.

• *Nutritional content per serving of 4 to 6 large shrimp: Cals: 102; % of cals. from fat: 46; Fat: 7g; Sat. fat: 1g; Carbs: 2g; Fiber: 0.4g; Sugars: 0.4g; Cholesterol: 109mg; Protein: 7g; Sodium: 211mg*

# savory stuffed mushrooms

These tasty bites filled with fresh spinach, shiitake mushrooms, and chopped walnuts make a light and lovely hors d'oeuvre for any occasion.

**SERVES 8 / 2 APIECE**

1 TABLESPOON OLIVE OIL
1 CUP FINELY CHOPPED ONIONS
½ CUP FINELY CHOPPED SHIITAKE MUSHROOMS
2 GARLIC CLOVES, MINCED
KOSHER SALT AND FRESHLY GROUND BLACK PEPPER
1 CUP WELL-DRAINED AND FINELY CHOPPED FRESH SPINACH
   OR BABY SPINACH
½ CUP CHOPPED GROUND WALNUTS
16 LARGE BUTTON MUSHROOMS, STEMMED AND LEFT WHOLE

1. Preheat the oven to 350°F.
2. Heat the oil in a large skillet and cook the onions, shiitake mushrooms, and garlic, stirring, for 10 minutes. Season to taste with salt and pepper. Stir in the spinach and cook for about 5 minutes. Remove from the heat and stir in the walnuts. Finely chop the mixture again.
3. Stuff each button mushroom with the filling and put on a baking sheet. Bake for about 10 minutes. Serve warm.

• *Nutritional content per serving: 8 servings per recipe: Cals.: 81; % of cals. from fat: 74; Fat: 7g; Sat. fat: 1g; Carbs: 5g; Fiber: 1g; Sugars: 2g; Cholesterol: 0mg; Protein: 2g; Sodium: 155mg*

# lemon-rosemary chicken bites

These delightful chicken bites will never fail to please your guests.

**SERVES 12 /2 APIECE**

½ CUP SAFFLOWER OIL
2 TABLESPOONS FRESH LEMON JUICE
2 TABLESPOONS FRESHLY GRATED LEMON ZEST
2 TEASPOONS CHOPPED FRESH ROSEMARY
1 TABLESPOON CHOPPED FRESH FLAT-LEAF PARSLEY
KOSHER SALT AND FRESHLY GROUND BLACK PEPPER
1½ POUNDS BONELESS, SKINLESS CHICKEN BREAST,
   CUT INTO TWENTY-FOUR 1½-INCH PIECES

1. In a medium bowl, whisk together 4 tablespoons of the oil, lemon juice, lemon zest, rosemary, parsley, and salt and pepper to taste. Add the chicken pieces and stir to coat. Cover and refrigerate for 2 to 3 hours. Remove and drain chicken.

2. In a large sauté pan, heat 2 tablespoons of the oil until smoking. Sear the chicken pieces on each side until cooked through, about 2 minutes per side. Transfer the chicken to a plate lined with paper towels and drain well. Repeat with the remaining oil and chicken pieces. Serve warm with toothpicks.

• *Nutritional content per serving: 12 servings per recipe: Cals.: 46; % of cals. from fat: 20; Fat: 1g; Sat. fat: 0.2g; Carbs: 0g; Fiber: 0g; Sugars: 0g; Cholesterol: 21mg; Protein: 9g; Sodium: 121mg*

# A Cocktail Party for Friends

Toasted Party Nuts
(page 3)

Seviche with Avocados & Tomatoes
(page 4)

Pickled Party Shrimp
(page 6)

Pita Pizza Wedges with Mozzarella,
Tomatoes, & Arugula
(page 11)

Lemon-Rosemary Chicken Bites
(page 8)

Herbed Goat Cheese Spread
with Oven-Baked Pita Crisps
(pages 18–19)

Crostini with Sautéed Spinach & Ricotta Cheese
(page 25)

# pita pizza wedges with mozzarella, tomatoes, & arugula

Pita triangles make a tasty base for these mini pizzas topped with mozzarella cheese and chopped fresh tomatoes and arugula. This is a good snack to make for hungry kids as well as sophisticated adults.

**SERVES 8 / 4 APIECE**

4 MEDIUM PLUM TOMATOES, FINELY DICED
1 SMALL RED ONION, FINELY MINCED
1 TABLESPOON EXTRA-VIRGIN OLIVE OIL
KOSHER SALT AND FRESHLY GROUND BLACK PEPPER
4 WHOLE WHEAT OR WHITE PITAS, 7 INCHES IN DIAMETER
2 CUPS SHREDDED LOW-FAT MOZZARELLA CHEESE
½ CUP CHOPPED FRESH ARUGULA

1. Preheat the oven to 350°F.
2. Put the tomatoes and their juice, onion, olive oil, and salt and pepper to taste in a medium bowl and stir. Let the mixture sit for about 15 minutes.
3. Using a sharp knife, split the pitas all the way around the perimeter so you have two circles. Cut each round into 4 wedges. Put the wedges on a baking sheet and top each with a spoonful of cheese. Bake until the pitas begin to brown and crisp and the cheese is melted, about 8 to 10 minutes. Remove from the oven and let them cool a bit.
4. Spoon a bit of the tomato mixture over each pita wedge and top with chopped arugula. Serve warm.

• *Nutritional content per serving: 8 servings per recipe: Cals.: 169; % of cals. from fat: 35; Fat: 7g; Sat. fat: 3g; Carbs: 19g; Fiber: 2g; Sugars: 3g; Cholesterol: 15mg; Protein: 11g; Sodium: 417mg*

# handmade spicy tortilla chips

These chips are quite light-tasting with a very rich corn flavor. They are delicious with Fresh Tomato Salsa (page 15) or Black Bean Salsa (page 16), or Guacamole (page 13).

**SERVES 8 / 4 APIECE**

1 TABLESPOON EXTRA-VIRGIN OLIVE OIL
PINCH OF KOSHER SALT
1 TEASPOON PAPRIKA
PINCH OF CAYENNE PEPPER
FOUR 6-INCH CORN TORTILLAS, EACH CUT INTO 8 SMALL WEDGES

1. Preheat the oven to 325°F.

2. Put the olive oil, salt, paprika, and cayenne pepper in a large bowl and mix well.

3. Add the tortilla wedges to the oil and spice mixture. Toss well to coat. Put them on a baking sheet in a single layer. Bake until crisp, about 15 minutes. Set aside to cool a bit and serve.

• *Nutritional content per serving: 4 chips per serving: Cals.: 42; % of cals. from fat: 45; Fat: 2g; Carbs: 6g; Fiber: 1g; Sugars: 0.2g; Cholesterol: 0mg; Protein: 1g; Sodium: 35mg*

# guacamole

There are a number of ways to make guacamole, but like many recipes, the simplest one is often the best. Be sure the avocados are perfectly ripe and that you don't mash them too aggressively, since the guacamole should retain a slightly chunky texture.

**MAKES ABOUT 2 CUPS**

2 RIPE AVOCADOS, PITTED, HALVED, AND COARSELY CHOPPED
1 TABLESPOON FRESH LIME JUICE
½ RIPE TOMATO, COARSELY CHOPPED
½ RED ONION, DICED
PINCH OF GROUND CUMIN
KOSHER SALT

1. Scoop the avocado into a bowl. Add the lime juice and mash lightly with a fork.
2. Gently mix in the tomato, onion, and cumin and continue to mash. Season to taste with the salt and mash again until well mixed but not too smooth. Serve at once.

• *Nutritional content per serving: 8 servings per recipe: Cals.: 84; % of cals. from fat: 79; Fat: 7g; Carbs: 5g; Fiber: 4g; Sugars: 1g; Cholesterol: 0mg; Protein: 1g; Sodium: 100mg*

**GOOD GUACAMOLE!**

Avocados are cholesterol-free, sodium-free, and low in saturated fat. Research shows that avocados offer the following phytonutrients that contribute to overall health and wellness:

**Lutein**—a carotenoid associated with healthy eye, heart, and prostate function.

**Vitamin E**—a powerful antioxidant that neutralizes free radicals.

**Glutathione**—functions as an antioxidant like vitamin E.

**Beta-sitosterol**—helps maintain healthy cholesterol levels.

**Monounsaturated fats**—heart-healthy fat that can lower LDL (bad) cholesterol and maintain HDL (good) cholesterol when substituted for saturated fat.

**Folate**—helps promote healthy cell and tissue development.

**Potassium**—helps balance the body's electrolytes.

## SALSAS

Translated from Spanish, salsa means "sauce," but these days the term is so familiar that we rarely think of its Mexican roots when we make it. Salsas can be made with a variety of healthy ingredients and are excellent alternatives to high-calorie dips and sauces. They can be served with chips and raw vegetables, and are also delicious as accompaniments to grilled or pan-seared seafood, chicken, pork, and beef.

Salsas are also terrific party fare because they can be made a day or two ahead of time and can be served chilled or at room temperature.

# fresh tomato salsa

This basic tomato salsa pairs well with chips and raw vegetables as well as with grilled chicken.

**MAKES ABOUT 3½ CUPS**

2 LARGE TOMATOES, SEEDED AND COARSELY CHOPPED
1 MEDIUM RED BELL PEPPER, STEMMED, SEEDED, AND FINELY DICED
1 MEDIUM YELLOW BELL PEPPER, STEMMED, SEEDED, AND FINELY DICED
1 MEDIUM RED ONION, CUT INTO ¼-INCH DICE
1 TEASPOON EXTRA-VIRGIN OLIVE OIL
1 TABLESPOON FRESH LIME JUICE
2 TABLESPOONS CHOPPED FRESH FLAT-LEAF PARSLEY
2 TABLESPOONS CHOPPED FRESH CILANTRO (OPTIONAL, SEE NOTE)
1 TEASPOON CHILI POWDER
1 TEASPOON GROUND CUMIN
PINCH OF CAYENNE PEPPER
DASH OF HOT SAUCE
KOSHER SALT AND FRESHLY GROUND BLACK PEPPER

1. Combine the tomatoes, peppers, and onion in a large bowl. Add the olive oil and lime juice and toss gently to mix.

2. Add the parsley, cilantro, if using, chili powder, cumin, cayenne pepper, and hot sauce and toss gently. Season to taste with salt and pepper. Cover and refrigerate for at least 2 hours or until well chilled.

3. Serve chilled or at room temperature. The salsa will keep, covered, in the refrigerator for up to 2 days.

• *Nutritional content per serving: 8 servings per recipe: Cals.: 28; % of cals. from fat: 26; Fat: 1g; Sat. fat: 0g; Carbs: 5g; Fiber: 3g; Sugars: 3g; Cholesterol: 0mg; Protein: 1g; Sodium: 106mg*

**Note:** Fresh cilantro, also known as coriander, has a pungent flavor that lends itself well to spicy foods. It may be an acquired taste for some, so it's best to check with your guests before using it in any recipe. If omitting cilantro in this recipe, substitute with additional fresh parsley or fresh chives.

# black bean salsa

Hearty black beans, garden-fresh tomatoes, and spicy jalapeños combine to make a delicious salsa to serve as a dip or condiment, or to spoon into warm corn tortillas.

**MAKES ABOUT 3½ CUPS**

1 (15.5-OUNCE) CAN BLACK BEANS, WELL RINSED AND DRAINED
1 LARGE TOMATO, SEEDED AND COARSELY CHOPPED
2 GARLIC CLOVES, MINCED
1 LARGE OR 2 SMALL JALAPEÑO PEPPERS, SEEDED AND MINCED
2 SCALLIONS, TRIMMED AND MINCED (WHITE AND LIGHT GREEN PARTS)
½ RED ONION, CUT INTO ¼-INCH DICE
2 TABLESPOONS CHOPPED FRESH CILANTRO (OPTIONAL)
1 TEASPOON CHILI POWDER
1 TEASPOON GROUND CUMIN
1 TEASPOON EXTRA-VIRGIN OLIVE OIL
1 TEASPOON RED WINE VINEGAR
1 TEASPOON FRESH LEMON JUICE
KOSHER SALT AND FRESHLY GROUND BLACK PEPPER

1. Combine the beans, tomato, garlic, peppers, scallions, onion, cilantro, if using, chili powder, and cumin in a large bowl and stir gently. Add the olive oil, vinegar, and lemon juice and stir gently again. Season to taste with salt and pepper.

2. Cover and refrigerate for at least a day before serving. The salsa will keep in the refrigerator for up to 3 days.

• *Nutritional content per serving: 8 servings per recipe: Cals.: 60; % of cals. from fat: 14; Fat: 1g; Sat. fat: 0g; Carbs: 10g; Fiber: 3g; Sugars: 2g; Cholesterol: 0mg; Protein: 4g; Sodium: 100mg*

# A Weekend Afternoon Lunch

## Black Bean Salsa
(page 16)

## Handmade Spicy Tortilla Chips
(page 12)

## Grilled Mexican Chicken Salad
(page 82)

## Mixed Greens

## Creamy Lemon-Rice Pudding
(page 209)

## Iced Mint & Lemon Verbena Tea
(page 233)

# oven-baked pita crisps

Oven-Baked Pita Crisps, made with mixed spices and olive oil, are very good accompaniments to all types of dips and spreads as well as for soups. They can be made ahead of time and keep very well when stored in an airtight container.

**MAKES ABOUT 3 DOZEN CRISPS**

1 TABLESPOON FENNEL SEEDS, FINELY GROUND
1 TEASPOON GARLIC POWDER
½ TEASPOON PAPRIKA
PINCH OF CAYENNE PEPPER
PINCH OF SEA SALT
3 PITAS (6 TO 7 INCHES IN DIAMETER), SPLIT HORIZONTALLY
    AND CUT INTO 2-INCH WEDGES
2 TEASPOONS OLIVE OIL

1. Preheat the oven to 350°F.
2. Mix the fennel seeds, garlic powder, paprika, cayenne pepper, and salt together.
3. Put the spice mixture and the pita pieces in a large bowl. Drizzle with the olive oil, then toss together well. Place on a baking sheet and bake until crisp, about 10 minutes.

• *Nutritional content per 4 chip serving: Cals.: 68; % of cals. from fat: 19; Fat: 1g; Sat. fat: 0g; Carbs: 12g; Fiber: 1g; Sugars: 0.5g; Cholesterol: 0mg; Protein: 2g; Sodium: 134mg*

# herbed goat cheese spread

This tangy, goat cheese spread is made with fresh tarragon, parsley, and scallions, but you can use just about any fresh herb in this recipe. When the goat cheese is combined with drained plain low-fat yogurt, it gives it a lovely consistency. For a delightful hors d'oeuvre, serve the spread with grilled bread or Oven-Baked Pita Crisps (page 18) and crudités.

**MAKES ABOUT 1½ CUPS**

6 OUNCES PLAIN LOW-FAT YOGURT
8 OUNCES MILD GOAT CHEESE, AT ROOM TEMPERATURE
2 TEASPOONS FINELY CHOPPED FRESH TARRAGON
2 TABLESPOONS FINELY CHOPPED FRESH FLAT-LEAF PARSLEY
2 TABLESPOONS TRIMMED AND FINELY MINCED SCALLIONS
   (WHITE AND LIGHT GREEN PARTS)
2 TABLESPOONS FINELY MINCED RED ONION
KOSHER SALT AND FRESHLY GROUND BLACK PEPPER

1.  Line a sieve with a coffee filter and place it over a bowl. Spoon the yogurt into the filter and let it drain for about 1 hour at room temperature, or overnight in the refrigerator.

2.  In a medium bowl, gently mash the goat cheese with a fork to soften. Add the tarragon, parsley, scallions, and red onion and work them in with the fork. Season to taste with salt and pepper, mashing to make a smooth, well-blended spread.

3.  Add the yogurt and mix until well blended. If you are not serving at once, cover and refrigerate. The spread can be made up to 2 days ahead of time. Bring it to room temperature before serving.

• *Nutritional content per serving: 12 servings per recipe: Cals.: 61; % of cals. from fat: 62; Fat: 4g; Sat. fat: 3g; Carbs: 2g; Fiber: 0g; Sugars: 1g; Cholesterol: 20mg; Protein: 4g; Sodium: 159mg*

**LOWER-FAT CHEESES**

Some of the best lower-fat cheeses are French-style goat cheese and French and Greek feta cheeses made from sheep's milk. Other excellent choices are part-skim cheeses such as mozzarella, ricotta, and Neufchâtel (reduced-fat cream cheese). Reduced-fat versions of Monterey Jack, Swiss, and cheddar cheeses are also available. They generally contain one-third less fat than regular cheese.

# tofu, scallion, & ginger dip

Most dips and spreads taste better when they are made a few hours ahead of time to allow their full flavors to develop. This dip made with silken or soft tofu is no exception. This type of tofu can be found in the refrigerated section of some groceries, health-food stores, and organic markets.

**MAKES ABOUT 1½ CUPS**

1 POUND SILKEN OR SOFT TOFU, DRAINED
3 SCALLIONS, TRIMMED AND MINCED (WHITE AND LIGHT GREEN PARTS)
1 TABLESPOON MINCED FRESH GINGER
2 GARLIC CLOVES, THINLY SLICED
1 TEASPOON CHOPPED FRESH FLAT-LEAF PARSLEY
2 TABLESPOONS LOW-SODIUM SOY SAUCE
½ TEASPOON TOASTED SESAME OIL

1. Put the tofu, scallions, ginger, garlic, parsley, soy sauce, and sesame oil in a food processor or blender. Blend until smooth.

2. Cover and refrigerate for 1 hour before serving. The dip will keep, covered, in the refrigerator for up to 3 days.

• *Nutritional content per serving: 12 servings per recipe: Cals.: 25; % of cals. from fat: 47; Fat: 4g; Sat. fat: trace; Carbs: 1g; Fiber: 0g; Sugars: 1g; Cholesterol: 0mg; Protein: 2g; Sodium: 96mg*

# herbed yogurt & horseradish dip

This fresh and delicious dip is fabulous to serve with a platter of colorful vegetables, such as strips of red, yellow, and green peppers, sliced cucumbers, and baby carrots.

**MAKES ABOUT 1½ CUPS**

½ CUP PLAIN LOW-FAT YOGURT
½ CUP LOW-FAT COTTAGE CHEESE
1 GARLIC CLOVE, THINLY SLICED
2 TABLESPOONS PREPARED HORSERADISH
¼ CUP CHOPPED FRESH FLAT-LEAF PARSLEY
2 TABLESPOONS MINCED FRESH CHIVES
KOSHER SALT AND FRESHLY GROUND BLACK PEPPER

1.  Line a sieve with a coffee filter and place it over a bowl. Spoon the yogurt into the filter and let it drain for about 1 hour at room temperature, or overnight in the refrigerator.

2.  Put the yogurt and cottage cheese in a food processor or blender and blend until smooth. Add the garlic, horseradish, parsley, chives, and salt and pepper to taste and blend again. Taste and adjust the seasonings, if necessary.

3.  Cover and refrigerate for 1 hour before serving. The dip will keep, covered, in the refrigerator for up to 3 days.

• *Nutritional content per serving: 12 servings per recipe: Cals.: 16; % of cals. from fat: 11; Fat: trace; Sat. fat: trace; Carbs: 2g; Fiber: 0g; Sugars: 1g; Cholesterol: 1mg; Protein: 2g; Sodium: 113mg*

# crostini

Crostini are thin slices of bread that are baked in the oven until nicely toasted then rubbed with garlic and brushed with olive oil. They are delicious with any number of toppings and make a terrific hors d'oeuvre for almost any type of party.

**SERVES 10 / 2 APIECE**

TWENTY ¼-INCH SLICES FROM A BAGUETTE
3 LARGE GARLIC CLOVES, PEELED AND HALVED
ABOUT ¼ CUP OLIVE OIL, FOR BRUSHING

1. Preheat the oven to 400°F.
2. Arrange the bread slices in a single layer on a baking sheet and bake until golden brown and crispy, about 5 minutes. Remove from the heat. Rub the garlic halves over one side of the bread and brush lightly with the olive oil.
3. Serve the crostini with desired toppings.

• *Nutritional content per serving: 10 servings per recipe: Cals.:166; % of cals. from fat: 12; Fat: 12g; Sat. fat: 2g; Carbs: 13g; Fiber: 1g; Sugars: trace; Cholesterol: 0mg; Protein: 2g; Sodium: 153mg*

# crostini with lemon hummus

Delicious lemony hummus is easy to make and tastes great as a spread for crostini.

**ABOUT 1½ CUPS HUMMUS (FOR 20 TOASTS)**

1 (15- TO 16-OUNCE) CAN CHICKPEAS, DRAINED
3 TABLESPOONS FRESH LEMON JUICE
1½ TABLESPOONS TAHINI (SESAME PASTE)
1 GARLIC CLOVE, THINLY SLICED
1 TEASPOON GROUND CUMIN
1 TEASPOON PAPRIKA
½ TEASPOON CAYENNE PEPPER
KOSHER SALT AND FRESHLY GROUND BLACK PEPPER
20 CROSTINI SLICES
ROASTED RED PEPPERS, THINLY SLICED, FOR GARNISH

1. Put the chickpeas, lemon juice, tahini, garlic, cumin, paprika, cayenne pepper, and salt and pepper to taste in a food processor and blend until fairly smooth and fluffy, scraping down the sides of the bowl once or twice. Transfer to a bowl, cover and refrigerate for at least 1 hour. The hummus will keep, covered, in the refrigerator for up to 3 days. Bring to room temperature before serving.

2. Spread the hummus on crostini, garnish with a red pepper strip, and serve.

• *Nutritional content per serving of hummus: 10 servings per recipe: Cals.: 67; % of cals. from fat: 24; Fat: 2g; Sat. fat: trace; Carbs: 11g; Fiber: 2g; Sugars: 2g; Cholesterol: 0mg; Protein: 3g; Sodium: 365mg*

# crostini with
# roasted eggplant spread

When eggplant is slow-roasted in the oven it develops a subtle smoky flavor. It's very good to serve on crostini. It also works well as a dip with flatbread.

**ABOUT 1½ CUPS SPREAD (FOR 20 TOASTS)**

1 LARGE EGGPLANT
½ TEASPOON GROUND CUMIN
1 TABLESPOON TAHINI (SESAME PASTE)
1 MEDIUM PLUM TOMATO, SEEDED AND FINELY CHOPPED
1 TABLESPOON FRESH LEMON JUICE
1 GARLIC CLOVE, THINLY SLICED
KOSHER SALT AND FRESHLY GROUND BLACK PEPPER
1 TEASPOON EXTRA-VIRGIN OLIVE OIL
20 CROSTINI SLICES
FRESH FLAT-LEAF PARSLEY SPRIGS, FOR GARNISH

1. Preheat the oven to 425°F. Lightly oil a baking sheet.

2. Cut the eggplant in half lengthwise and score the flesh with a knife in several places. Place the eggplant, cut sides down, on the prepared baking sheet and bake until the eggplant is very soft and starts to collapse, 30 to 40 minutes. Set aside to cool.

3. When cool enough to handle, scoop out the eggplant flesh and transfer to a medium bowl, discarding as many seeds as possible. Add the cumin and tahini, and mash with a fork into a coarse puree. Stir in the chopped tomato, lemon juice, garlic, and salt and pepper to taste. The spread will keep, covered, in the refrigerator for up to 3 days. Bring to room temperature before serving.

4. Just before serving, stir in the olive oil; taste and adjust the seasonings, if necessary. Spread the eggplant mixture on crostini, garnish with parsley, and serve.

• *Nutritional content per serving of eggplant spread: 10 servings per recipe: Cals.: 38; % of cals. from fat: 33; Fat: 1g; Sat. fat: trace; Carbs: 7g; Fiber: 2g; Sugars: 2g; Cholesterol: 0mg; Protein: 1g; Sodium: 120mg*

# crostini with sautéed spinach & ricotta cheese

This elegant version of crostini is excellent party fare for the holidays. It looks and tastes great.

**MAKES 20 TOASTS / 2 APIECE**

1 TABLESPOON OLIVE OIL
3 CUPS BABY SPINACH
PINCH OF DRIED CHILE FLAKES
KOSHER SALT AND FRESHLY GROUND BLACK PEPPER
20 CROSTINI SLICES
¾ CUP LOW-FAT RICOTTA CHEESE
ROASTED RED PEPPERS, THINLY SLICED, FOR GARNISH

1. Heat the olive oil in a skillet or sauté pan. Add the spinach and sauté for 1 minute. Add the chile flakes and salt and pepper to taste and sauté until the spinach is wilted, about 3 minutes. Transfer to a bowl.

2. Spread the crostini with the cheese and a spoonful of warm spinach. Garnish with a red pepper strip and serve.

• *Nutritional content per serving: 10 servings per recipe: Cals.: 28; % of cals. from fat: 58; Fat: 2g; Sat. fat: 1g; Carbs: 1g; Fiber: trace; Sugars: 1g; Cholesterol: 5mg; Protein: 2g; Sodium: 155mg*

# healthy crostini

They're appetizers, hors d'oeuvres, sandwiches—say hello to crostini, the tasty finger food that brings together what we all love about sandwiches without the drawbacks of too much bread and fatty fillings. Don't hesitate to use various types of bread: thinly sliced, small rounds of whole grain and mixed grain varieties, sourdough, or herb-flavored loafs. In addition to the recipes in this section, here are some suggestions for preparing these party favorites.

### ASPARAGUS & PARMESAN
Make sure to break off tough ends of asparagus, peel the stalks and steam the tips until tender enough to bite through easily—but don't overcook. Place on toasts and sprinkle with a dusting of freshly grated Parmesan.

### FENNEL & OLIVES
Shave the fennel so that it's onion-skin thin (you can use the wide slot on a four-sided grater or a mandoline) and remove pits from oil-cured olives, if necessary, and dice. Top with fennel first, then the olives.

### ROASTED EGGPLANT, BELL PEPPERS, & MOZZARELLA
Brush thin slices of eggplant and bell peppers lightly with olive oil and roast until softened and browned. Top the toasts with a slice of each and a piece of salt-free mozzarella.

### ROASTED ZUCCHINI
The key here, too, is to use very thin slices of zucchini. Toss them in olive oil and add a pinch of salt–and roast in a hot oven until the edges begin to brown. Spoon onto the toasts.

### CHICKPEAS & TOMATO
These are superfoods, packed with good-for-you nutrients and fiber. Puree the chickpeas and a dash of fresh lemon juice in a food processor until fairly smooth. Finely dice a tomato. Top the toasts with the chickpea spread and tomatoes. Drizzle with a bit of olive oil, if desired.

### WHITE BEANS & SPINACH
Puree cooked white beans (canned are okay) and steamed and well-drained chopped spinach in a food processor. Top the toasts with the spread and two or three whole beans and sprinkle with a bit of finely diced flat-leaf parsley.

# New Year's Day
# Open House

**Crostini with Lemon Hummus**
(page 23)

**Vegetable Platter**
**with Herbed Yogurt & Horseradish Dip**
(page 21)

Savory Stuffed Mushrooms
(page 7)

Spicy Vegetarian Chili
with Assorted Condiments
(page 154)

Jicama, Orange, & Watercress Salad
(page 62)

Lemon–Poppy Seed Cake
(page 199)

Oatmeal Raisin Cookies
(page 208)

Fresh Fruit Platter

❧

chapter two **soups**

C hilled or piping hot—as an appetizer or the main course—soup is one of the most versatile dishes and is a great addition to any party menu. Served chilled in big-handled mugs at poolside, as an entrée in front of a roaring fire, or ladled into dainty china bowls for a first course of a dinner party, it offers you a chance to make a strong culinary statement—while you simplify cooking and serving a meal. The Gazpacho with Grilled Shrimp & Corn is a feast for the taste buds and the Vegetable & White Bean Minestrone needs nothing more than a piece of good bread and a glass of wine to make a complete meal.

# cool cucumber, yogurt, & dill soup

Cool and refreshing cucumber soup is a cinch to make and it's just the thing to serve as a starter on a warm summer evening. Apple cider vinegar adds a bit of tang to the mellow flavors of cucumbers, yogurt, and dill in this recipe.

**SERVES 6**

4 POUNDS CUCUMBERS (6 TO 7 MEDIUM),
    PEELED, SEEDED, AND CHOPPED
1 SMALL ONION, SLICED
3 TABLESPOONS CIDER VINEGAR
3 TABLESPOONS COARSELY CHOPPED FRESH DILL
6 CUPS 99% FAT-FREE LOW-SODIUM CHICKEN BROTH
2 CUPS WATER
½ CUP MILK
KOSHER SALT AND FRESHLY GROUND BLACK PEPPER
1 TO 1½ CUPS PLAIN LOW-FAT YOGURT
CHOPPED FRESH DILL, FOR GARNISH
CUCUMBER SLICES, FOR GARNISH

1. In a large stockpot, combine the cucumbers, onion, vinegar, and dill. Add the broth and water, bring to a boil, stirring, over high heat. Lower the heat to medium–low and simmer, partially covered, until the cucumbers are very soft, about 30 minutes. Set aside to cool until barely warm.

2. Transfer to a food processor fitted with a metal blade or a blender (this will have to be done in batches). Puree until smooth. Transfer to a bowl and stir in the milk. Season to taste with salt and pepper. Cover and chill for at least 4 hours or overnight.

3. Spoon the yogurt into shallow, chilled soup bowls. Taste and adjust the seasonings, and then ladle the soup over the yogurt. Garnish with dill and cucumber slices and serve.

• *Nutritional content per serving: 6 servings per recipe: Cals.: 58; % of cals. from fat: 19; Fat: 1g; Sat. fat:0; Carbs: 8g; Fiber: 2g; Sugars: 5g; Cholesterol: 2mg; Protein: 4g; Sodium: 222mg*

**COOL CUCUMBERS**

Cucumbers are available year-round at markets and greengrocers, but they taste best in summer, particularly if they are homegrown or bought from a local farmer. Look for slender, green cucumbers—the giant ones are full of tasteless seeds—and slice them for salads or sandwiches, chop them for dips, or use them to make soup. The most common variety is the smooth cucumber. It's also easy to find bumpy Kirbys (also called pickling cucumbers) and long seedless cucumbers (also called English or hothouse cucumbers).

# gazpacho
# with grilled shrimp & corn

This summery gazpacho, made with ripe, red tomatoes and peppers and charcoal-grilled fresh corn and shrimp always wins raves. It is best to make the gazpacho base a day ahead of time to allow the flavors of the soup time to blend and intensify.

**SERVES 6**

4 MEDIUM TOMATOES, CORED AND DICED

2 MEDIUM RED BELL PEPPERS, STEMMED, SEEDED,
   AND FINELY CHOPPED

2 MEDIUM CUCUMBERS, PEELED, SEEDED,
   AND COARSELY CHOPPED

1 MEDIUM RED ONION, COARSELY CHOPPED

2 GARLIC CLOVES, THINLY SLICED

2 CUPS LOW-FAT CHICKEN BROTH

⅓ CUP SHERRY VINEGAR

DASH OF TABASCO SAUCE

PINCH OF CAYENNE PEPPER

2 TABLESPOONS CAPERS, DRAINED

KOSHER SALT AND FRESHLY GROUND BLACK PEPPER

½ POUND (ABOUT 18) LARGE SHRIMP, PEELED AND DEVEINED

2 EARS FRESH CORN, PEELED

CORN OIL, FOR BRUSHING

¼ CUP CHOPPED FRESH FLAT-LEAF PARSLEY, FOR GARNISH

1. Place the tomatoes, peppers, cucumbers, onion, garlic, broth, vinegar, Tabasco, cayenne pepper, capers, and salt and pepper to taste in a large bowl and stir to mix well.

2. Transfer half of the mixture to a food processor fitted with a metal blade or a blender and puree until smooth. Return to the bowl and mix well. Taste and adjust the seasonings, if necessary. Cover and refrigerate overnight.

continued

**3.** Prepare a gas or charcoal grill. Brush the shrimp and corn with corn oil. When the fire is medium-hot, and the coals are covered with a light coating of ash and glow deep red, grill the shrimp, turning often, until cooked through, about 5 minutes (see Note). Grill the corn, turning often, until lightly browned all over, 8 to 10 minutes.

**4.** When cool enough to handle, scrape the corn from the cobs and add to the gazpacho.

**5.** Ladle the soup into 6 shallow, chilled soup bowls. Top each serving with 3 of the grilled shrimp, sprinkle with the parsley, and serve at once.

**Note:** A grill wok or a grill wok topper works very well for cooking the shrimp over the fire.

• *Nutritional content per serving: 6 servings per recipe: Cals.: 137; % of cals. from fat: 11; Fat: 2; Sat. fat: trace; Carbs: 22g; Fiber: 4g; Sugars: 8g; Cholesterol: 58mg; Protein: 12g; Sodium: 676mg*

# yellow pepper gazpacho

This robust and colorful version of gazpacho is full of fresh yellow bell peppers, cucumbers, red onions, and ripe tomatoes. It's very refreshing and tasty topped with thin slices of avocado and a dollop of yogurt.

**SERVES 6**

4 MEDIUM YELLOW BELL PEPPERS, SEEDED, DEVEINED,
  AND FINELY CHOPPED
2 MEDIUM CUCUMBERS, PEELED, SEEDED,
  AND COARSELY CHOPPED
4 LARGE RIPE TOMATOES, CORED AND CUT INTO WEDGES
1 MEDIUM RED ONION, PEELED AND COARSELY CHOPPED
2 CLOVES GARLIC, THINLY SLICED
2 CUPS LOW-FAT CHICKEN BROTH
⅓ CUP BALSAMIC VINEGAR
2 TABLESPOONS CAPERS, DRAINED
AVOCADO SLICES, FOR GARNISH
PLAIN LOW-FAT YOGURT, FOR GARNISH

1. Place the bell peppers, cucumbers, tomatoes, onion, garlic, broth, vinegar, and capers in a large bowl and stir to mix well.

2. Transfer half of the mixture to a food processor fitted with a metal blade or a blender and puree until smooth. This will have to be done in batches.

3. Return the puree to the bowl and mix well. Taste and adjust the seasoning, if necessary. Cover and refrigerate for at least 4 hours. Stir the mixture well before serving.

4. Ladle into chilled soup mugs and top each serving with avocado slices a spoonful of yogurt.

• *Nutritional content per serving: 6 servings per recipe (without garnish): Cals.: 76; % of cals. from fat: 8; Fat: 1g; Sat. fat: 0; Carbs: 17g; Fiber 3g; Sugars: 10g; Cholesterol: 1mg; Protein: 3g; Sodium: 422mg*

**PARTY PERFECT**

When serving soup as a first course at a sit-down dinner, place the filled bowls on a serving plate at each seat before your guests sit down. For a buffet or outdoors, you can place an attractive pot on a warmer with a ladle and arrange large mugs alongside for self-service.

# A Summer Evening Dinner

Cool Cucumber, Yogurt, & Dill Soup
(page 33)

Grilled Swordfish
with Spicy Mango Salsa
(page 147)

Roasted Stuffed Peppers
with Fresh Corn & Zucchini
(page 152)

Chickpea Salad with Chopped
Tomatoes, Cucumbers, & Fennel
(page 69)

Mixed Greens with Lemon Vinaigrette

Grilled Peaches
with Red Wine Sauce
(page 217)

❧

# roasted autumn vegetable soup

When farm-fresh acorn squash and carrots are slow-roasted with onions and a pinch of butter and sugar, they can be transformed into a fragrant and creamy soup. A dash of cayenne pepper and hot paprika adds a nice kick to it too. This beautiful soup is very good for you since squash and carrots are loaded with beta-carotene and vitamins C and E, as well as fiber and potassium.

**SERVES 6**

2 SMALL BUTTERNUT SQUASH (ABOUT 3 POUNDS),
   SEEDED AND HALVED
4 CARROTS, PEELED AND CUT INTO ½-INCH PIECES
1 ONION, QUARTERED
1 TABLESPOON UNSALTED BUTTER
1 TABLESPOON LIGHT BROWN SUGAR
4 CUPS 99% FAT-FREE CHICKEN BROTH
KOSHER SALT AND FRESHLY GROUND BLACK PEPPER
1 CUP WATER
½ TEASPOON GROUND GINGER
PINCH OF CAYENNE PEPPER
PINCH OF HOT PAPRIKA
2 TABLESPOONS SNIPPED FRESH CHIVES, FOR GARNISH

1. Preheat the oven to 375°F.
2. Put the squash halves, cut side up, in a large roasting pan and distribute the carrots and onions around them. Dot the vegetables with butter and sprinkle with the brown sugar. Pour 1 cup of the broth over the vegetables and season to taste with salt and pepper. Cover with aluminum foil and roast until the squash is tender, about 1 hour.
3. Let the squash cool in the pan until cool enough to handle. Scoop the squash flesh from the skins and transfer the flesh to a large soup pot; discard the skins. Add the carrots, onions, any pan juices, the water, and the remaining 3 cups of broth. Bring to a boil over high heat, reduce the heat to medium, stir in the ginger, and simmer, uncovered, for about 15 minutes until the flavors blend.

**4.** Transfer the soup to a food processor or blender and puree until smooth. This will have to be done in batches. Return it to the pot. At this point, the soup can be refrigerated, covered, for 2 or 3 days, or frozen for up to a month.

**5.** Bring the soup to a gentle boil over medium-high heat, stirring well. Season to taste with cayenne pepper, paprika, and additional salt and pepper and cook until piping hot. To serve, ladle into 6 soup bowls and garnish with the chives.

*• Nutritional content per serving: 6 servings per recipe: Cals.: 124; % of cals. from fat: 18; Fat: 3g; Sat. fat: 1; Carbs: 25g; Fiber: 3g; Sugars: 8g; Cholesterol: 6mg; Protein: 3g; Sodium: 885mg*

## THE POWER COOK

More fun, less fuss. That's the secret of serving soup at a winter dinner gathering or for a summer lunch by the pool. As the main course, soup is a way to make your job as a host much easier. Prepared well ahead of time, it cuts down on last-minute rushing around in the kitchen, and frees you up to enjoy making the accompanying dishes such as the Grilled Garlic Shrimp, White Bean, & Arugula Salad on page 75, or the Orange Angel Food Cake with Fresh Strawberry Rhubarb Sauce on page 201. You can also prepare a double batch of soup without much more effort and freeze it for your family to enjoy again later. And if you are concerned about watching your weight, it's been shown that eating soup such as the Wild Mushroom Consommé (on page 43) as a first course can help reduce your overall calorie intake and promotes weight loss.

# carrot & ginger soup

This velvety, ginger-spiked soup, made with fresh carrots, is very rich in vitamin A. Serve it as a lovely first course for an autumn dinner party.

**SERVES 6**

1 TABLESPOON OLIVE OIL
3 MEDIUM ONIONS, COARSELY CHOPPED
5 CUPS LOW-SODIUM VEGETABLE BROTH
1 CUP WATER
6 LARGE CARROTS, PEELED AND DICED
3 TABLESPOONS FINELY GRATED FRESH GINGER
1 TEASPOON GROUND CINNAMON
1 TEASPOON GROUND CORIANDER
PINCH OF CAYENNE PEPPER
KOSHER SALT AND FRESHLY GROUND BLACK PEPPER
½ CUP MINCED FRESH CHIVES, FOR GARNISH

1. In a large nonreactive stockpot, heat the olive oil over medium heat. Add the onions and cook, stirring, until softened, about 5 minutes.

2. Add the broth, water, carrots, and 2 tablespoons of the grated ginger. Bring to a boil, reduce the heat, and simmer, partially covered, until the carrots are tender, about 20 minutes. Remove the pot from the heat and let the soup cool for about an hour.

3. Transfer the soup to a food processor fitted with a metal blade or a blender. Add the remaining ginger, cinnamon, and coriander and puree until very smooth (this will have to be done in batches). Season with the cayenne pepper and salt and pepper to taste.

4. Return the soup to the pot and reheat gently. Garnish each serving with fresh chives and serve at once.

• *Nutritional content per serving: 6 servings per recipe: Cals.: 78; % of cals. from fat: 33; Fat: 3g; Sat. fat: trace; Carbs: 12g; Fiber: 3g; Sugars: 7g; Cholesterol: 0mg; Protein: 1g; Sodium: 200mg*

# wild mushroom consommé

This dark, woodsy broth is a light and sophisticated prologue to a winter dinner. It is best to make it a day ahead to give the mushrooms, vegetables, and peppercorns time to steep so that the rich flavors infuse the broth.

**SERVES 6**

1 POUND SHIITAKE MUSHROOMS WITH STEMS, HALVED

½ POUND WHITE MUSHROOMS, STEMMED AND HALVED

½ POUND CREMINI MUSHROOMS, STEMMED AND HALVED

1 WHITE ONION, COARSELY CHOPPED

2 CARROTS, COARSELY CHOPPED

1 RIB CELERY, COARSELY CHOPPED

6 BLACK PEPPERCORNS

6 GREEN PEPPERCORNS

6 RED PEPPERCORNS

½ CUP CHOPPED FRESH FLAT-LEAF PARSLEY

4 QUARTS WATER

KOSHER SALT AND FRESHLY GROUND BLACK PEPPER

4 WHITE MUSHROOMS, THINLY SLICED, FOR GARNISH

LEMON SLICES, FOR GARNISH

6 TABLESPOONS SNIPPED FRESH CHIVES, FOR GARNISH

1. In a large nonreactive stockpot, combine the shiitake, white, and cremini mushrooms, onion, carrots, celery, peppercorns, and parsley with the water and season to taste with salt and pepper. Bring to a boil over medium-high heat. Reduce the heat, skim any foam that rises to the top, and simmer for 25 to 30 minutes until reduced by half. Set aside to cool and then cover and refrigerate for at least 8 hours or overnight.

2. Strain the soup through a sieve or a strainer lined with cheesecloth. Discard the solids and return the broth to the pot and heat over medium-high heat until very hot. Adjust the seasonings with salt and pepper.

3. Ladle into soup bowls and garnish with the white mushroom slices, lemon slices, and fresh chives. Serve immediately.

• *Nutritional content per serving: 6 servings per recipe: Cals.: 60; % of cals. from fat: 6; Fat: trace; Sat. fat: 0g; Carbs: 14g; Fiber: 3g; Sugars: 7g; Cholesterol: 0mg; Protein: 3g; Sodium: 224mg*

**CLEANING MUSHROOMS**

Mushrooms absorb water and so should never be soaked in water or left under running water for more than a few seconds, if at all. In most cases, they can be cleaned simply by wiping with a damp cloth.

# vegetable & white bean minestrone

This classic soup—comprised of vegetables, white beans, and pasta—is rich in fiber, vitamins, calcium, and iron, and is immensely satisfying. It makes a delicious comfort-food supper when served with a salad of dark, leafy greens and Italian bread.

**SERVES 6**

2 TABLESPOONS OLIVE OIL

1 LARGE ONION, COARSELY CHOPPED

2 LARGE CELERY RIBS, COARSELY CHOPPED

2 CARROTS, PEELED AND COARSELY CHOPPED

2 GARLIC CLOVES, THINLY SLICED

3 CUPS VEGETABLE BROTH

3 CUPS WATER

1 (16-OUNCE) CAN PLUM TOMATOES, WITH LIQUID,
  COARSELY CHOPPED

2 RUSSET POTATOES, PEELED AND DICED

PINCH OF DRIED OREGANO

PINCH OF CELERY SEEDS

½ POUND GREEN BEANS, TRIMMED AND CUT INTO 1-INCH SLICES

2 CUPS THINLY SLICED CABBAGE

1 (15-OUNCE) CAN CANNELLINI OR GREAT NORTHERN BEANS,
  RINSED AND DRAINED

½ CUP PENNETTE, DITALI, OR OTHER SMALL TUBULAR PASTA

½ CUP CHOPPED FRESH BASIL

¼ CUP CHOPPED FRESH FLAT-LEAF PARSLEY

KOSHER SALT AND FRESHLY GROUND BLACK PEPPER

⅓ CUP FRESHLY GRATED PARMESAN CHEESE

**1.** Heat the olive oil in a large stockpot over medium heat. Add the onion, celery, carrots, and garlic and cook over medium heat, stirring occasionally, until the vegetables begin to soften, about 5 minutes. Add the broth, water, tomatoes, potatoes, oregano, and celery seeds. Bring to a boil over high heat, reduce the heat to low and cook, covered, for 10 minutes.

continued

**2.** Add the green beans, cabbage, beans, and pasta. Simmer, uncovered, over medium heat until the vegetables and pasta are tender, about 15 minutes. (The soup can be made several hours ahead of time. Reheat before serving, adding additional liquid if necessary.)

**3.** Stir in the basil and parsley and season with salt and pepper to taste. Ladle into bowls and serve with Parmesan cheese.

• *Nutritional content per serving: 6 servings per recipe: Cals.: 251; % of cals. from fat: 28; Fat: 8g; Sat. fat: 2g; Carbs: 36g; Fiber: 8g; Sugars: 9g; Cholesterol: 7mg; Protein: 10g; Sodium: 1045mg*

## THE HEALTH CONNECTION

This hearty entrée soup is a bowl of goodness. The beans are packed with fiber—this recipe offers you about 25% of your daily recommended intake, just from the beans. Add the vegetables and you are well on your way to a full day's portion. The recommendation is to eat 25 to 30 grams of fiber per day. People with diabetes need the same amount of fiber as everyone else. The benefits? Fiber may help you control glucose levels and lower cholesterol levels. One study showed that people eating 21 grams per day had 12% less coronary heart disease compared to those eating 5 grams daily. The soup provides ample calcium, a mineral that is also helpful in weight loss and heart health, in addition to its bone-strengthening powers. The beans also fill many other dietary requirements—including 32% daily value of folate and 9% daily value of potassium—and are very high in protein. Beans are high in carbohydrates, however. They contribute about 12 grams of carbs per serving. The vegetables add another intense dose (see the nutritional analysis at the end of the recipe), so you want to take that into account when figuring how to handle your post-dinner glucose levels.

# A Winter Afternoon Lunch

Caesar Salad
with Lemon Vinaigrette & Water Chestnuts
(page 55)


Vegetable & White Bean Minestrone
(page 45)


Oven-Baked Pita Crisps
(page 18)


Gingerbread–Spice Cake
(page 204)

# seafood chowder

Serve this fantastic chowder, which is chock-full of clams, mussels, and shrimp with salad and crusty bread for a very impressive main course.

**SERVES 6**

2 TABLESPOONS OLIVE OIL

1 LARGE ONION, THINLY SLICED

3 GARLIC CLOVES, THINLY SLICED

1 CUP DRY WHITE WINE OR 99% FAT-FREE CHICKEN BROTH

1 CUP WATER

1 (28-OUNCE) CAN PLUM TOMATOES, WITH LIQUID,
    COARSELY CHOPPED

6 SPRIGS FRESH FLAT-LEAF PARSLEY

¼ TEASPOON DRIED THYME

¼ TEASPOON FENNEL SEEDS

2 PINCHES OF SAFFRON

1 DOZEN LITTLENECK CLAMS, RINSED

2 POUNDS MUSSELS, WELL-SCRUBBED, RINSED, AND DE-BEARDED

1 POUND (ABOUT 32 TO 36) LARGE SHRIMP

½ CUP CHOPPED FRESH FLAT-LEAF PARSLEY, FOR GARNISH

**SHRIMP SHELLS**

The shrimp can be peeled and deveined or cooked with their shells on. The shrimp shells add more flavor to the broth.

1.  Heat the olive oil in a large stockpot over medium heat. Add the onion and garlic and cook, stirring, until softened and slightly golden, about 5 minutes. Add the wine or broth, water, and tomatoes. Cook over high heat until just boiling. Reduce the heat and add the parsley, thyme, fennel seeds, and saffron. Cook, uncovered, at a gentle simmer for 30 minutes, stirring occasionally. (The chowder base can be made ahead of time up to this point. Set aside until cool, then refrigerate, covered, for up to 3 days. It can also be frozen for up to 1 month.)

2.  Bring soup base to a rapid boil. Add clams, mussels, and shrimp and bring back to a boil. Cover tightly. Cook until clams and mussels open and shrimp turns pink; 8 to 10 minutes. Discard any shells that are unopened.

3.  Ladle the chowder into large soup bowls, garnish with parsley, and serve at once.

• *Nutritional content per serving: 6 servings per recipe: Cals.: 315; % of cals. from fat: 27; Fat: 9g; Sat. fat: 1g; Carbs: 15g; Fiber: 2g; Sugars: 11g; Cholesterol: 143mg; Protein: 36g; Sodium: 737mg*

# A Seafood Dinner

Vegetable Platter with
Herbed Yogurt & Horseradish Dip
(page 21)

Seafood Chowder
(page 48)

Mixed Greens with Oil & Vinegar

Yogurt, Blueberry,
& Toasted Walnut Parfaits
(page 215)

❧

# eat your colors

Soups can pack a nutritional powerhouse and the simplest way to make sure they do is to select as ingredients 3 to 5 differently colored foods. This is important because the colors indicate that the foods contain differing types and amounts of health-protecting antioxidants and other important chemicals. Recent studies have pointed to the possible ability of these color-related plant compounds to slow aging and protect the heart, mind, and digestive system from disease.

### RED
Tomatoes, especially when cooked, are the ruler of this category, delivering the most lycopene, a potent antioxidant. Other sources include apricots, guava, watermelon, papaya, and pink grapefruit.

### YELLOW & ORANGE
Yellow apples, apricots, cantaloupe, yellow figs, grapefruit, lemons, mangoes, nectarines, oranges, papayas, peaches, yellow pears, persimmons, pineapples, tangerines, yellow beets, butternut squash, carrots, yellow peppers, sweet corn, sweet potatoes, yellow tomatoes, and yellow winter squash contain carotenoids and bioflavonoids, efficient free-radical scavengers.

### WHITE
Bananas, dates, white peaches and nectarines, brown pears, cauliflower, garlic, ginger, jicama, mushrooms, onions parsnips, white-fleshed potatoes, shallots, turnips, and white corn contain allicin and selenium. Allicin is an antibiotic and antifungal chemical that is present in garlic and is touted for a whole roster of ailments, although it is not well proved. Selenium is a trace mineral that acts as an antioxidant and in the United States is found in breads and meats as well as fruits and vegetables.

### GREEN
Avocados, green grapes, kiwi, limes, green pears, artichokes, arugula, asparagus, broccoli, green beans, green cabbage, celery, cucumbers, endive, leafy greens, green onions, okra, peas, green pepper, spinach, watercress, and zucchini contain lutein, a carotenoid that helps protect the eyes, as well as a cornucopia of vitamins and minerals.

### BLUE
This category includes blackberries, blueberries, plums, purple grapes, raisins, purple cabbage, eggplant, purple peppers, and purple-fleshed potatoes. They contain the flavonoid called anthocyanin, which reduces inflammation and phenolics.

chapter three **salads**

# G

reens do not a salad make—or at least they are not the only way to make one! We love everyone's favorite, the Caesar salad, here made with an anchovy-free lemon vinaigrette. But there are also some very exciting twists combining a wide range of vegetables—from asparagus to cabbage and fennel to beets—and mixing them with grains, grilled meats and fish, and even nuts. These recipes transform the salad course from a place holder between an appetizer and an entrée into the highlight of any meal. As a main course, try the Grilled Garlic Shrimp, White Bean, & Arugula Salad, or Tabbouleh & Vegetable Salad. Or for an after-entrée serve Asparagus & Celery Salad with Walnut Dressing. Here's a course that adds enormous flavor—and (shhh!) is good for you too.

# caesar salad with lemon vinaigrette & water chestnuts

Romaine-based Caesar salad is now reputed to be America's most popular salad, and it's served in countless ways. This version is made with a creamy, light, lemony dressing; anchovies are optional. Chopped water chestnuts, instead of the usual croutons, add a tasty crunch to the salad.

**SERVES 6**

**VINAIGRETTE:**

2 GARLIC CLOVES, HALVED
1 TABLESPOON FRESH LEMON JUICE
1 TEASPOON WHITE WINE VINEGAR
½ CUP EXTRA-VIRGIN OLIVE OIL
2 TABLESPOONS MILK
KOSHER SALT AND FRESHLY GROUND BLACK PEPPER

1 MEDIUM HEAD ROMAINE LETTUCE,
    TOUGH OUTER LEAVES REMOVED, INNER LEAVES TORN IN HALF
½ CUP WATER CHESTNUTS, DRAINED AND HALVED
½ CUP FRESHLY GRATED PARMESAN CHEESE
ANCHOVIES, FOR GARNISH (OPTIONAL)

1.  To make the vinaigrette, put the garlic, lemon juice, and vinegar in a food processor. Process for about 30 seconds. With the motor running, slowly add the oil through the feed tube and process until thick. Turn off the machine, add the milk and salt and pepper to taste. Process again until well combined. The vinaigrette will keep, covered, in the refrigerator, for up to 2 days. Bring to room temperature and whisk well before serving.

2.  Put the lettuce in a large bowl. Add just enough vinaigrette to moisten the lettuce (there will be some dressing left over) and toss to coat. Add the water chestnuts, sprinkle with the cheese, and toss again. Taste and adjust the seasonings, if necessary. Serve at once from the bowl or arrange on individual plates. Garnish with anchovies, if desired.

• *Nutritional content per serving: 6 servings per recipe: Dressing: Cals.: 165; % of cals. from fat: 99; Fat: 18g; Sat. fat: 2g; Sodium: 198mg. Salad: Cals.: 49; % of cals. from fat: 48; Fat: 3g; Sat. fat:1g; Carbs: 4g; Fiber: 2g; Sugars: 1g; Cholesterol: 7mg; Protein: 4g; Sodium: 67mg*

**TURNING OVER A NEW LEAF**

When it comes to lettuce and other greens, the quality of the produce is the key to a beautiful and great tasting salad. Try to find the freshest greens possible, and opt for locally grown and/or organic romaine and mesclun whenever possible. And remember, never cut romaine—always tear it into serving-size pieces. Iceberg is the only lettuce you should take a knife to.

# greek salad with lemon-garlic vinaigrette

When we think of Greek salad we often imagine a bowl of pallid lettuce, chunky cucumbers, thick green pepper rings, and a few hunks of feta cheese. This revamped Greek salad is light and fresh, made with romaine lettuce, seedless cucumbers, roasted red peppers, and other excellent ingredients. This salad can be served as an entrée, or as a tasty side with grilled lamb, chicken, or seafood.

**SERVES 6**

**LEMON-GARLIC VINAIGRETTE:**
1 TEASPOON DIJON MUSTARD
1 TABLESPOON FRESH LEMON JUICE
1 GARLIC CLOVE, FINELY MINCED
¼ CUP EXTRA-VIRGIN OLIVE OIL
PINCH OF SUGAR
KOSHER SALT AND FRESHLY GROUND BLACK PEPPER

1 SMALL HEAD ROMAINE LETTUCE, TOUGH OUTER LEAVES
   REMOVED, INNER LEAVES TORN INTO 1-INCH PIECES
1 SEEDLESS CUCUMBER, PEELED, QUARTERED LENGTHWISE,
   AND CUT INTO ½-INCH CUBES
4 RIPE PLUM TOMATOES, EACH CUT INTO 8 WEDGES
½ RED ONION, THINLY SLICED
¼ CUP CHOPPED FRESH FLAT-LEAF PARSLEY
8 OUNCES FETA CHEESE, CRUMBLED
½ CUP KALAMATA OLIVES
1 ROASTED RED PEPPER, THINLY SLICED
¼ CUP CHOPPED FRESH MINT LEAVES, FOR GARNISH

**1.** To make the vinaigrette, whisk together the mustard, lemon juice, and garlic in a small bowl. Slowly add the olive oil, whisking constantly, until thickened. Season to taste with the sugar, salt, and pepper. The vinaigrette will keep, covered, in the refrigerator for up to 2 days. Bring to room temperature before using.

2. In a large bowl, toss together the lettuce leaves, cucumber, and 2 tablespoons of the vinaigrette and set aside.

3. In another bowl, toss the tomatoes, onion, and parsley with 2 tablespoons of the vinaigrette and set aside.

4. Arrange the greens among 6 salad plates or on a large platter. Spoon the tomato mixture on top of the greens. Top with the feta cheese and a few olives. Arrange the red peppers over the salad and garnish with the mint.

• *Nutritional content per serving: 6 servings per recipe: Dressing: Cals.: 83; % of cals. from fat: 99; Fat: 18g; Sat. fat: 1g; Sodium: 214mg. Salad: Cals.: 143 ; % of cals. from fat: 69; Fat: 10g; Sat. fat: 6g; Carbs: 9g; Fiber: 3g; Sugars: 5g; Cholesterol: 34mg; Protein: 7g; Sodium: 533mg*

## SALAD GREENS

Here are three types of greens that work very well on their own or in any combination.

**Mild Greens**
Bibb Lettuce: soft, small heads with large, pale green outer leaves
Boston Lettuce: fluffy, loose heads with soft, pale green leaves
Iceberg Lettuce: compact, crisp heads with very pale green leaves
Loose Leaf Lettuce: large, soft medium green or red leaves
Oak Leaf Lettuce: curly edged, tender red leaves
Romaine Lettuce: long, crisp, medium green leaves
Spinach: deep green, heart-shaped leaves, crisp if large and tender if small

**Peppery Greens**
Arugula/Rocket: tender, very dark green leaves
Watercress: small, shiny, dark green leaves with stems

**Bitter Greens**
Chicory/Curly Endive: elongated, crisp, medium green, curly leaves
Endive: small, elongated heads with pale green leaves with yellow or red edges
Escarole: large, soft green leaves with pale centers; cook outer dark leaves
Frisée: smaller, milder, paler green cousin to chicory
Radicchio: ruby red leaves in small, tight, round heads

# asparagus & tomato salad with mustard-dill vinaigrette

This salad, made with garden-fresh asparagus and cherry tomatoes, is a very refreshing starter. The garlicky vinaigrette recipe, which can be made well ahead of time, yields a generous amount—use any left over to drizzle over steamed vegetables.

**SERVES 6; MAKES 1 CUP OF VINAIGRETTE**

2½ TO 3 POUNDS SLENDER FRESH ASPARAGUS

**MUSTARD-DILL VINAIGRETTE:**
1 GARLIC CLOVE, SLICED
½ SMALL YELLOW ONION, COARSELY CHOPPED
¼ CUP CHOPPED FRESH DILL
1 TABLESPOON DIJON MUSTARD
¼ CUP BALSAMIC VINEGAR
⅓ CUP WATER
½ CUP SAFFLOWER OIL
KOSHER SALT AND FRESHLY GROUND BLACK PEPPER

6 CUPS FRESH MIXED SALAD GREENS
1 CUP CHERRY TOMATOES, HALVED
¼ CUP THINLY SLICED ALMONDS, LIGHTLY TOASTED

1. Cut or break off the tough woody ends of the asparagus stalks and discard.

2. In a large saucepan or skillet, bring enough lightly salted water to cover the asparagus to a boil over high heat. Add the asparagus, reduce the heat to simmer, and cook just until tender, 3 to 5 minutes. Drain well. Chill the asparagus for an hour.

3. To make the vinaigrette, put the garlic, onion, dill, mustard, vinegar, water, oil, and salt and pepper to taste in a food processor fitted with a steel blade or a blender and blend until smooth. The vinaigrette will keep, covered, in the refrigerator for up to a week.

*continued*

**THE CLEVER COOK**

Ever wonder how
restaurants make their
asparagus such a vibrant
green color? The chef's
trick is to make sure you
cook it in salted water.
If you want to reduce
your salt intake, you can
quickly rinse the
asparagus after cooking.

**4.** Toss the greens and tomatoes together with about ¼ cup of the vinaigrette. Toss the asparagus in a separate bowl with about 2 tablespoons of the vinaigrette, then place over the salad greens. Sprinkle with the almonds and add a bit more vinaigrette, if desired. (You will have about ½ cup of vinaigrette left over.) Serve at once.

• *Nutritional content per serving: 6 servings per recipe: Dressing: Cals.: 173; % of cals. from fat: 94; Fat: 18g; Sat. fat: 1g; Sodium: 254mg. Salad: Cals.: 45; % of cals. from fat: 60; Fat: 3g; Sat. fat: trace; Carbs: 4g; Fiber: 2g; Sugars: 2g; Cholesterol: 0mg; Protein: 2g; Sodium: 9mg*

# asparagus & celery salad with walnut dressing

The tastes complement each other beautifully in this refreshing salad.

**SERVES 6**

2½ POUNDS SLENDER FRESH ASPARAGUS
3 CELERY RIBS, CUT INTO ¼-INCH PIECES ON THE DIAGONAL
6 TABLESPOONS WALNUT OIL
2 TABLESPOONS FRESH LEMON JUICE
2 TABLESPOONS FINELY MINCED RED ONION
KOSHER SALT AND FRESHLY GROUND BLACK PEPPER
3 TABLESPOONS CHOPPED WALNUTS

**1.** Cut or break off the tough ends of the asparagus stalks and discard.

**2.** In a large saucepan or skillet, bring enough lightly salted water to cover the asparagus to a boil over high heat. Add the asparagus, reduce the heat to simmer, and cook just until tender, 3 to 5 minutes. Drain well. Put the asparagus and celery in a shallow serving bowl or platter.

**3.** To make the dressing, whisk together the oil, lemon juice, onion, and salt and pepper to taste in a small bowl. Pour the dressing over the vegetables and toss lightly to coat. Marinate, covered, at room temperature for at least an hour.

**4.** Sprinkle the walnuts over the salad and serve.

• *Nutritional content per serving: 6 servings per recipe: Dressing: Cals.: 146; % of cals. from fat: 98; Fat: 16g; Sat. fat: 2g; Sodium: 195mg. Salad: Cals.: 25; % of cals. from fat: 48; Fat: trace; Sat. fat: 0g; Carbs: 5g; Fiber: 2g; Sugars: 2g; Cholesterol: 0mg; Protein: 2g; Sodium: 32mg*

# Mother's Day Dinner

Asparagus & Tomato Salad
with Mustard-Dill Vinaigrette
(page 58)


Pan-Seared Salmon
with Lemon-Soy Sauce
(page 144)


Roasted Sweet Potatoes
with Lime & Cilantro
(page 180)


Sautéed Garlic & Orange Spinach
(page 177)


Yogurt, Blueberry,
& Toasted Walnut Parfaits
(page 215)

# jicama, orange, & watercress salad

This light and refreshing salad is excellent served as part of a summer buffet. It is also very good when paired with grilled or roasted chicken.

**SERVES 6**

3 CUPS JICAMA, PEELED AND CUT INTO THICK STRIPS,
   2½ INCHES IN LENGTH
2 TABLESPOONS FRESH LIME JUICE
3 MEDIUM ORANGES, PEELED AND CUT INTO SEGMENTS
1 BUNCH WATERCRESS, RINSED AND STEMMED
⅓ CUP RED WINE VINEGAR
½ TEASPOON GROUND CUMIN
KOSHER SALT AND FRESHLY GROUND BLACK PEPPER
⅓ CUP EXTRA-VIRGIN OLIVE OIL
1 HEAD BOSTON LETTUCE

1. Place the jicama strips in a large bowl. Add the lime juice and toss well. Add the orange segments and watercress and toss again.

2. To make the vinaigrette, stir together the vinegar, cumin, and salt and pepper to taste in a small bowl. Whisk in the olive oil until thickened. Taste and adjust the seasonings. Pour over the jicama mixture, and toss. Taste and adjust the seasonings, and gently toss again.

3. Separate the lettuce leaves and arange in a shallow serving bowl. Spoon the jicama salad over them. Serve immediately.

  • *Nutritional content per serving: 6 servings per recipe: Dressing: Cals.: 108; % of cals. from fat: 99; Fat: 12g; Sat. fat: 2g; Sodium: 108mg. Salad: Cals.: 72; % of cals. from fat: 4; Fat: trace; Sat. fat: 0g; Carbs: 17g; Fiber: 6g; Sugars: 9g; Cholesterol: 0mg; Protein: 2g; Sodium: 16mg*

# red cabbage, pepper, & onion slaw with orange-cumin vinaigrette

Serve this sweet and spicy slaw, which is subtly flavored with orange and lime juice, as a tasty side dish for a summer barbecue.

**SERVES 8 TO 10**

1 HEAD RED CABBAGE, CORED AND THINLY SLICED
1 RED BELL PEPPER, SEEDED, DEVEINED, AND THINLY SLICED
1 RED ONION, THINLY SLICED

**ORANGE-CUMIN VINAIGRETTE:**
2 TABLESPOONS RED WINE VINEGAR
3 TABLESPOONS ORANGE JUICE
1 TABLESPOON FRESH LIME JUICE
⅓ CUP LOW-FAT MAYONNAISE
2 TABLESPOONS LOW-FAT PLAIN YOGURT
1 TEASPOON GROUND CUMIN
¼ CUP EXTRA-VIRGIN OLIVE OIL

KOSHER SALT AND FRESHLY GROUND BLACK PEPPER
¼ CUP CHOPPED FRESH FLAT-LEAF PARSLEY

1.  Put the cabbage, bell pepper, and onion in a very large bowl. Toss together until well combined.

2.  To make the vinaigrette, mix together the vinegar, orange juice, and lime juice in a medium bowl. Gently stir in the mayonnaise, yogurt, and cumin until well combined. Whisk in the olive oil until the vinaigrette is creamy and thickened and all of the oil has been incorporated.

3.  Pour the vinaigrette over the cabbage mixture and toss well. Add salt and pepper to taste and mix well again. Garnish with chopped parsley. Cover and chill the slaw until ready to serve.

4. Taste and adjust the seasonings, if necessary, and serve.

• *Nutritional content per serving: 8 servings per recipe: Dressing: Cals.: 83; % of cals. from fat: 81 Fat: 8g; Sat. fat: 1g; Sodium: 242mg. Salad: Cals.: 38; % of cals. from fat: 7; Fat: trace; Sat. fat: 0g; Carbs: 9g; Fiber: 3g; Sugars: 6g; Cholesterol: 0mg; Protein: 2g; Sodium: 13mg*

Science has found that there is a lot to treasure about the walnut. The oil has been shown to lower triglycerides, which may reduce the risk of coronary heart disease. The Food and Drug Administration says there is a reliable indication that eating 1.5 ounces of walnuts a day reduces the risk of coronary heart disease. And a recent study found that eating 8 to 10 walnuts a day can reduce bad LDL cholesterol by 10% in people with type 2 diabetes. Seems the nuts are rich in the polyunsaturated fatty acids—especially the essential omega-3 fats— that you need to reduce the risk of heart disease. The simple, low-carb snack may also improve sensitivity to insulin.

# endive, beet, & walnut salad

Roasted beets and endive taste and look great together, especially when they're drizzled with walnut oil and topped with a bit of blue cheese and chopped walnuts. This salad makes a lovely lunch or dinner appetizer.

**SERVES 6**

6 MEDIUM BEETS (ABOUT 2 POUNDS), TRIMMED
3 TABLESPOONS WALNUT OIL
KOSHER SALT AND FRESHLY GROUND BLACK PEPPER
3 HEADS ENDIVE
⅓ CUP CRUMBLED BLUE OR ROQUEFORT CHEESE
⅓ CUP CHOPPED WALNUT PIECES

1.  Preheat the oven to 375°F.
2.  Wrap the beets tightly in foil to make 2 packages (3 beets in each) and roast until tender, about 1¼ hours.
3.  Carefully unwrap the beets and, when just cool enough to handle, slip off the skins and remove the stems. Cut the beets into ¼-inch rounds and transfer to a bowl. Add 1 tablespoon of the walnut oil to the beets. Season to taste with salt and pepper and toss gently.
4.  Separate the endive leaves. Arrange them on a platter or divide among 6 salad plates. Drizzle the endive with another tablespoon of the oil. Spoon the beets over the endive and sprinkle with the cheese and walnuts. Drizzle the salad with the remaining oil, add some additional pepper, if desired, and serve.

• *Nutritional content per serving: 6 servings per recipe: Cals.: 230; % of cals. from fat:66; Fat: 17g; Sat. fat: 4g; Carbs: 14g; Fiber: 6g; Sugars: 7g; Cholesterol: 14mg; Protein: 8g; Sodium: 556mg*

# Birthday Dinner Party

Toasted Party Nuts
(page 3)

Endive, Beet, & Walnut Salad
(page 64)

Grilled Lamb Chops
with Tarragon-Mustard Sauce
(page 133)

Sautéed Carrots with Black Olives
(page 170)

Roasted Cauliflower
(page 167)

Orange Angel Food Cake
with Fresh Strawberry Rhubarb Sauce
(page 201)

# wild rice, apricot, & pecan salad

This wonderfully crunchy salad is good to serve for a holiday dinner or
buffet. Look for good packaged rice, such as Texmati and Wild Rice Blend,
to add to the wild rice.

**SERVES 8**

1 CUP WILD RICE
1 CUP TEXMATI AND WILD RICE BLEND
2 TABLESPOONS FRESH LEMON JUICE
1 TABLESPOON CIDER VINEGAR
1 TABLESPOON LOW-SODIUM SOY SAUCE
½ CUP EXTRA-VIRGIN OLIVE OIL
½ CUP DRIED APRICOTS, COARSELY CHOPPED
½ CUP PECANS, TOASTED AND COARSELY CHOPPED (SEE NOTE)
½ CUP CHOPPED FRESH FLAT-LEAF PARSLEY
KOSHER SALT AND FRESHLY GROUND BLACK PEPPER
2 BUNCHES WATERCRESS, RINSED AND STEMMED

1.  Cook the rice according to package directions and drain. Transfer to
a large bowl, sprinkle with lemon juice, and toss.

2.  Whisk the cider vinegar, soy sauce, and olive oil together until well
blended. Pour over the rice and toss well to combine. Add the apricots,
pecans, parsley, and salt and pepper to taste and toss again. Taste and adjust
the seasonings, if necessary. Refrigerate the salad if not serving immediately.

3.  Bring the salad to room temperature before serving. To serve, arrange
the watercress on a large platter and spoon the salad over it.

**Note**: To toast the pecans, spread them on a baking sheet and toast them
in a preheated 350°F oven or toaster oven until golden brown and fragrant,
4 to 5 minutes. Shake the pan once or twice for even toasting. Slide the
nuts off the baking sheet as soon as they reach the desired color to stop the
cooking. Let them cool.

• *Nutritional content per serving: 8 servings per recipe: Cals.: 357; % of cals. from fat: 49; Fat: 20g;
Sat. fat: 2g; Carbs: 41g; Fiber: 5g; Sugars: 9g; Cholesterol: 0mg; Protein: 8g; Sodium: 208mg*

# winter fruit salad
# with walnuts & goat cheese

This salad, which is an updated version of the classic Waldorf Salad, is made with mixed greens, apples, and pears, and topped with lemony vinaigrette, goat cheese, and toasted walnuts. It is a lovely starter for an autumn or winter meal.

**SERVES 6**

2 HEADS ENDIVE

2 BUNCHES WATERCRESS, RINSED AND STEMMED

1 CUP (ABOUT 3 OUNCES) FRESH MIXED SALAD GREENS

1 MEDIUM UNPEELED RED APPLE, CORED
AND CUT INTO 1-INCH PIECES

1 MEDIUM UNPEELED GRANNY SMITH APPLE,
CORED AND CUT INTO 1-INCH PIECES

1 UNPEELED BOSC PEAR, CORED
AND CUT INTO 1-INCH PIECES

1 TABLESPOON DIJON MUSTARD

1 TABLESPOON WHITE WINE VINEGAR

1 TEASPOON FRESH LEMON JUICE

½ CUP EXTRA-VIRGIN OLIVE OIL

½ CUP WALNUT HALVES, LIGHTLY TOASTED (SEE NOTE)

2 OUNCES FRESH GOAT CHEESE, CRUMBLED (OPTIONAL)

KOSHER SALT AND FRESHLY GROUND BLACK PEPPER

1. Tear the endive leaves in half and place in a large bowl. Add the watercress, salad greens, chopped apples, and chopped pear and toss to combine.

2. To make the vinaigrette, whisk the mustard, vinegar, and lemon juice together in a small bowl. Slowly add the olive oil, whisking constantly, until the vinaigrette thickens.

3. Toss about ⅓ cup of the vinaigrette with the salad and heap the salad onto a platter or individual salad plates. Sprinkle the walnut halves and crumbled cheese, if using, over the top. Drizzle the salad with the remaining vinaigrette, if you wish. Season to taste with salt and pepper and serve immediately.

**Note:** To toast the walnuts, spread them on a baking sheet and toast them in a preheated 350°F oven or toaster oven until golden brown and fragrant, about 5 minutes. Shake the pan once or twice for even toasting. Slide the nuts off the baking sheet as soon as they reach the desired color to stop the cooking. Let them cool.

*• Nutritional content per serving: 6 servings per recipe: Dressing: Cals.: 163; % of cals. from fat: 99 Fat: 18g; Sat. fat: 2g; Sodium: 60mg. Salad: Cals.: 149; % of cals. from fat: 53; Fat: 9g; Sat. fat: 2g; Carbs: 16g; Fiber: 5g; Sugars: 9g; Cholesterol: 16mg; Protein: 25g; Sodium: 264mg*

# chickpea salad with chopped tomatoes, cucumbers, & fennel

Loaded with fresh vegetables, herbs, and spices, this terrific salad is just the thing to serve to a hungry crowd. It's okay to use canned chickpeas, if you're pressed for time, but dried ones retain their firmness and give this salad an especially good, crunchy texture.

**SERVES 8**

4 CUPS COOKED CHICKPEAS OR 2 (19-OUNCE) CANS CHICKPEAS, RINSED AND DRAINED

2 LARGE RIPE TOMATOES, COARSELY CHOPPED

2 LARGE UNPEELED CUCUMBERS, SEEDED AND DICED

2 SMALL FENNEL BULBS, TRIMMED AND DICED

½ CUP CHOPPED FRESH FLAT-LEAF PARSLEY

2 SMALL RED ONIONS, COARSELY CHOPPED

½ CUP CHOPPED FRESH MINT

⅓ CUP FRESH LEMON JUICE

⅓ CUP 99% FAT-FREE CHICKEN BROTH

4 TABLESPOONS EXTRA-VIRGIN OLIVE OIL

2 TEASPOONS GROUND CUMIN

2 TEASPOONS PAPRIKA

PINCH OF CAYENNE PEPPER

KOSHER SALT AND FRESHLY GROUND BLACK PEPPER

*continued*

1. In a large mixing bowl, toss together the chickpeas, tomatoes, cucumbers, fennel, parsley, onions, and mint.

2. To make the dressing, whisk together the lemon juice, broth, oil, cumin, paprika, cayenne pepper, and salt and pepper to taste in a small bowl. Pour the dressing over the salad and toss to mix well. Let the salad stand for at least an hour or refrigerate for up to 4 hours or overnight.

3. Before serving, taste and adjust the seasonings. You may want to refresh the salad with a bit of olive oil and lemon juice. Serve chilled or at room temperature.

• *Nutritional content per serving: 8 servings per recipe: Cals.: 246; % of cals. from fat: 34; Fat: 10g; Sat. fat: 1g; Carbs: 34g; Fiber: 9g; Sugars: 9g; Cholesterol: 0mg; Protein: 9g; Sodium: 232mg*

## FRIENDLY FATS

Salad dressings give us the opportunity to talk about good fats—essential fatty acids, monounsaturated and polyunsaturated. Monounsaturated and polyunsaturated fats are called "good" or "healthy" fats because they can lower your bad (LDL) cholesterol. Sources of monounsaturated fat include:

- Avocado
- Canola oil
- Nuts like almonds, cashews, pecans, and peanuts
- Olive oil and olives
- Peanut butter and peanut oil
- Sesame seeds

The American Diabetes Association recommends eating more monounsaturated fats and trying to eliminate trans fats and reduce saturated fats to 10% of your daily calorie intake. To include more monounsaturated fats, try to substitute olive or canola oil for butter, margarine, or shortening when cooking. Work with your dietitian to include healthy fats into your meal plan without increasing your total calories. Omega-3 fatty acids, found in these oils and in fish, also help protect your heart.

# tabbouleh & vegetable salad

**SERVES 8**

4 CARROTS, CUT INTO ½-INCH DISKS

4 PARSNIPS, CUT INTO ½-INCH DISKS

8 SHALLOTS, PEELED AND LEFT WHOLE

4½ TABLESPOONS EXTRA-VIRGIN OLIVE OIL

KOSHER SALT AND FRESHLY GROUND BLACK PEPPER

1 TEASPOON BALSAMIC VINEGAR

1½ CUPS BULGUR WHEAT

2 CUPS BOILING WATER

4 TABLESPOONS FRESH LEMON JUICE

4 SCALLIONS, TRIMMED AND MINCED (WHITE AND LIGHT GREEN PARTS)

1 CUP CHOPPED FRESH FLAT-LEAF PARSLEY

½ CUP CHOPPED FRESH MINT

FRESH FLAT-LEAF PARSLEY, FOR GARNISH

MINT LEAVES, FOR GARNISH

1.  Preheat the oven to 350°F.

2.  Put the carrots, parsnips, and shallots in a large roasting pan. Add 1½ tablespoons of the olive oil and salt and pepper to taste and toss well to coat the vegetables. Roast, stirring occasionally, until the vegetables are lightly browned and tender, about 50 minutes to an hour. Transfer to a medium bowl. Add the vinegar and toss together.

3.  Meanwhile, put the bulgur in a large bowl. Pour the boiling water over it. Cover the bowl with plastic wrap and let the bulgur steep until it has absorbed all of the water, about 30 minutes.

4.  Fluff the bulgur with a fork. Add 2 tablespoons of the lemon juice, 2 tablespoons of the olive oil, and salt and pepper to taste and mix well. Add the scallions, parsley, and mint and toss to combine. Add the remaining 2 tablespoons lemon juice and 1 tablespoon of the olive oil and toss again. Taste and adjust the seasonings, if necessary.

5.  Arrange the tabbouleh on a large platter. Spoon the roasted vegetables over it. Drizzle with a bit of lemon juice and olive oil, if desired. Garnish with parsley and mint leaves and serve at room temperature.

• *Nutritional content per serving: 8 servings per recipe: Cals.: 199; % of cals. from fat: 37; Fat: 8g; Sat. fat: 1g; Carbs: 29g; Fiber: 7g; Sugars: 3g; Cholesterol: 0mg; Protein: 4g; Sodium: 180mg*

## THE HEALTH CONNECTION

Tabbouleh is cracked bulgur wheat that is precooked. A serving of whole grain bulgur (½ cup, cooked) has more than 4 grams of dietary fiber and only 0.25 gram of fat. Diets high in soluble fiber have been shown to decrease the risk of cardiovascular disease by lowering LDL blood cholesterol levels. Bulgur also has very high levels of minerals such as calcium, phosphorus, and potassium and of antioxidants such as beta-carotene, lutein, and vitamin K.

Bulgur or cracked wheat is available packaged or in bulk in health food stores and in some supermarkets.

# poached salmon & watercress salad with dill vinaigrette

Basic poached salmon is an excellent recipe that every good cook should have in his or her repertoire, for it can be served in a number of healthy and delicious ways. There is nothing simpler or more elegant to serve than poached salmon fillets laced with fresh dill vinaigrette.

**SERVES 6**

**POACHED SALMON:**

6 SALMON FILLETS (ABOUT 6 OUNCES EACH), SKINNED

3 CUPS WATER

1 CUP DRY WHITE WINE

1 SMALL ONION, COARSELY CHOPPED

2 CARROTS, COARSELY CHOPPED

6 FRESH FLAT-LEAF PARSLEY SPRIGS

6 WHOLE PEPPERCORNS

4 WHOLE CLOVES

PINCH OF KOSHER SALT

2 CUPS (½ POUND), SNAP PEAS, RINSED AND TRIMMED

**VINAIGRETTE:**

1 TABLESPOON WHITE VINEGAR

1 TABLESPOON DIJON MUSTARD

½ CUP EXTRA-VIRGIN OLIVE OIL

2 TABLESPOONS CHOPPED FRESH DILL

KOSHER SALT AND FRESHLY GROUND BLACK PEPPER

2 BUNCHES WATERCRESS, RINSED AND STEMMED

2 TABLESPOONS EXTRA-VIRGIN OLIVE OIL

18 CHERRY TOMATOES, HALVED, FOR GARNISH

1.  Place the salmon fillets in a large shallow saucepan and cover with the water, wine, onion, carrots, parsley, peppercorns, cloves, and salt. Bring to a boil, reduce the heat and simmer, uncovered, for about 3 minutes for a pink center. Poach a bit longer, if desired, but do not overcook. Remove the fillets from the poaching liquid with a slotted spoon and drain. Set aside, or refrigerate if serving the salmon cold.

2.  Meanwhile, bring another pot of salted water to a boil, drop in the snap peas and boil, uncovered, until just tender and still bright green, 2 to 3 minutes. Drain and rinse immediately with cold water to stop the cooking.

3.  To make the vinaigrette, whisk the vinegar and mustard together in a small bowl. Slowly add the ½ cup olive oil, whisking until emulsified. Add the dill and salt and pepper to taste and whisk again until well combined.

4.  Toss the watercress with the 2 tablespoons olive oil and divide among 6 salad plates. Place a fillet over the watercress and garnish each plate with the snap peas and cherry tomatoes. Drizzle with vinaigrette and serve.

• *Nutritional content per serving: 6 servings per recipe: Cals.: 383; % of cals. from fat: 39; Fat: 15g; Sat. fat: 3g; Carbs: 5g; Fiber: 1g; Sugars: 3g; Cholesterol: 105mg; Protein: 37g; Sodium: 294mg Vinaigrette: Cals.: 208; % of cals. from fat: 98; Fat: 23g; Sat. fat: 3g; Sodium: 264mg*

**THE HEALTH CONNECTION**

Recent information indicates that you should stick with wild salmon and avoid farmed salmon; the farmed varieties have higher levels of toxins including mercury. In addition, wild salmon is 48% lower in fat than farmed salmon with almost the same amount of heart-healthy omega-3 oils that lower cholesterol and promote a healthy circulatory system. Fresh, fresh-frozen, or canned Alaska sockeye salmon provides the highest amount of omega-3 fatty acids of any fish—2.7 grams per 3.5-ounce (100-gram) portion. In this recipe the watercress offers a quarter of your daily values of vitamin C in a cup.

# grilled garlic shrimp, white bean, & arugula salad

Garlicky grilled shrimp, savory white beans, and pungent arugula impart a wonderful combination of tastes in this beautiful salad. This is lovely to serve as a main course for a summer lunch or dinner.

**SERVES 8**

1 CUP WHITE BEANS, PICKED OVER AND RINSED
2 CUPS 99% FAT-FREE CHICKEN BROTH
2 CUPS WATER
1 MEDIUM YELLOW ONION, PEELED
2 SMALL CARROTS, PEELED AND CUT IN HALF CROSSWISE
½ CUP EXTRA-VIRGIN OLIVE OIL
2 GARLIC CLOVES, THINLY SLICED
1 TABLESPOON CHOPPED FRESH ROSEMARY
2 TABLESPOONS DRY WHITE WINE
3 TABLESPOONS BALSAMIC VINEGAR
KOSHER SALT AND FRESHLY GROUND BLACK PEPPER
1½ POUNDS (ABOUT 32 TO 36 PER POUND) LARGE SHRIMP,
    PEELED AND DEVEINED
2 TABLESPOONS FRESH LEMON JUICE
1 BUNCH ARUGULA, RINSED AND STEMMED

    **1.** Put the beans in a medium bowl and add cold water to cover by about 2 inches. Soak for 6 to 8 hours or overnight. Change the water once or twice during soaking.

    **2.** Drain the beans and put them in a stockpot. Add the chicken broth, water, onion, and carrots. Bring to a boil over high heat, then reduce the heat, cover, and simmer, stirring occasionally, until just tender, 50 to 60 minutes. Be careful not to overcook or boil the beans.

continued

3. Drain and rinse the beans. Discard the onion and carrots. Place the beans in a large bowl.

4. Meanwhile, make the marinade for the shrimp. Put ¼ cup of the olive oil, garlic, rosemary, wine, 1 tablespoon of the vinegar, and salt and pepper to taste in a large glass or ceramic bowl and whisk together. Rinse the shrimp and pat them dry. Add the shrimp to the bowl and stir gently to coat with the marinade. Cover and refrigerate for 1 hour, stirring occasionally.

5. Prepare a gas or charcoal grill.

6. Remove the shrimp from the marinade, and arrange them on a grill wok or a grill wok topper. When the fire is medium-hot, and the coals are covered with a light coating of ash and glow deep red, grill until golden brown, about 5 to 7 minutes. Turn the shrimp once during cooking. (Alternatively, you may also cook the shrimp under the broiler in an aluminum foil–lined broiler tray.)

7. Add the shrimp to the beans, sprinkle with the lemon juice, add the arugula, and toss together.

8. Mix the remaining 2 tablespoons of the vinegar and the remaining ¼ cup olive oil together in a small bowl. Pour the mixture over the salad and toss. Taste and adjust the seasonings, if necessary, and toss again.

9. Serve chilled or at room temperature.

• *Nutritional content per serving: 8 servings per recipe: Cals.: 195; % of cals. from fat: 38; Fat: 8g; Sat. fat: 1g; Carbs: 10g; Fiber: 2g; Sugars: 2g; Cholesterol: 101mg; Protein: 16g; Sodium: 522mg*

# tuna niçoise salad

There are countless ways to make Tuna Niçoise Salad. In this version, it is made with grilled and marinated tuna, potatoes, a mix of green and yellow string beans, and tomatoes. It is then garnished with a chopped hard-cooked egg and—of course—niçoise olives. Serve this fantastic main course salad on a large platter for a festive lunch or dinner.

**SERVES 8**

2 TUNA STEAKS (8 OUNCES EACH), ABOUT 1 INCH THICK

KOSHER SALT AND FRESHLY GROUND BLACK PEPPER

½ CUP OLIVE OIL

4 GARLIC CLOVES, THINLY SLICED

8 SMALL RED POTATOES, SCRUBBED

½ POUND GREEN BEANS, ENDS TRIMMED

½ POUND YELLOW WAX BEANS, ENDS TRIMMED (SEE NOTE)

2 TABLESPOONS FRESH LEMON JUICE

1 GARLIC CLOVE, MINCED

1 LARGE TOMATO, COARSELY CHOPPED,
   OR 1 CUP HALVED CHERRY TOMATOES

½ CUP CHOPPED FRESH FLAT-LEAF PARSLEY

1 HARD-COOKED EGG, FINELY CHOPPED, FOR GARNISH

⅓ CUP NIÇOISE OLIVES, FOR GARNISH

1. Prepare a gas or charcoal grill. Season the tuna generously with salt and pepper, and when the fire is medium–hot, and the coals are covered with a light coating of ash and glow deep red, grill until it is seared on the outside but still rosy in the center, 3 to 4 minutes per side. (Alternatively, you may also cook the tuna under the broiler very close to the heat source.) Transfer the tuna to a nonreactive dish and add the olive oil and sliced garlic. Cover and refrigerate at least 6 hours or overnight.

continued

## CRISP AND FRESH

To crisp your greens, wash and then spin dry or drain on layers of paper towels. Tear off the floppy tops of the romaine or other greens and with your hands divide the leaves into pieces. Place in a large plastic bag with paper towels and refrigerate for 2 hours before making the salad.

**2.** Put the potatoes in a large saucepan and cover with salted water. Bring to a boil, lower the heat and simmer, covered, until tender, about 20 minutes. Drain, cool, and slice the potatoes. Set aside.

**3.** Bring another large saucepan of salted water to a boil and add the beans. Cook the beans until just crisp-tender, about 3 minutes. Drain the beans, rinse in cold water, and drain again. Set aside.

**4.** Drain the tuna, reserving 5 tablespoons of the oil, and discard the rest. Put the reserved oil in a large bowl and whisk together with the lemon juice and minced garlic. Add the potatoes, beans, tomato, and parsley. Season to taste with salt and pepper and toss well. Transfer the vegetables to a large platter.

**5.** Using a sharp knife, slice the tuna on the bias into thin slices. Arrange them over the vegetables. Sprinkle with the chopped egg and olives and serve.

**Note**: If you can't find yellow wax beans, use 1 pound of green beans.

• *Nutritional content per serving: 8 servings per recipe: Cals.: 282; % of cals. from fat: 35; Fat: 11g; Sat. fat: 1g; Carbs: 36g; Fiber: 15g; Sugars: 5g; Cholesterol: 48mg; Protein: 20g; Sodium: 282mg*

# A Wedding Shower Lunch

Gazpacho
with Grilled Shrimp & Corn
(page 34)

Tuna Niçoise Salad
(page 77)

Wild Rice, Apricot, & Pecan Salad
(page 67)

Salad Greens with Lemon Vinaigrette

Chocolate Chip Cake
(page 203)

# turkey salad
# with lime-ginger vinaigrette

Cold turkey, cucumbers, and scallions served over a bed of fresh greens and mint with vibrant vinaigrette make this a light and refreshing salad.

**SERVES 6**

**LIME-GINGER VINAIGRETTE:**

2 GARLIC CLOVES

1 JALAPEÑO PEPPER, SEEDED AND FINELY CHOPPED

2 TABLESPOONS SLICED GINGER

2 TABLESPOONS OYSTER SAUCE

2 TABLESPOONS SOY SAUCE

1 TABLESPOON RICE WINE VINEGAR

JUICE OF 1 LIME

1 TABLESPOON SUGAR

4 CUPS FRESH MIXED GREENS

1 CUP CHOPPED FRESH MINT

2 CUPS COOKED COLD TURKEY, CUT INTO STRIPS

⅔ CUP PEELED, SEEDED, AND JULIENNED CUCUMBER

1 SCALLION, TRIMMED AND FINELY CHOPPED
   (WHITE AND LIGHT GREEN PARTS)

FRESHLY GROUND BLACK PEPPER

**1.** To make the vinaigrette, place the garlic, pepper, ginger, oyster sauce, soy sauce, vinegar, lime, and sugar in a blender and blend until well combined. The vinaigrette will keep, covered, in the refrigerator for 1 week.

**2.** Place the greens and mint in a large bowl. Add 2 tablespoons of the vinaigrette and toss to coat the greens. Transfer to a platter.

**3.** Place the turkey, cucumber, and scallion in the bowl. Add 2 tablespoons of the vinaigrette and toss. Arrange the turkey mixture over the greens. Drizzle with the remaining vinaigrette, add fresh pepper to taste, and serve at once.

• *Nutritional content per serving: 6 servings per recipe: Cals.: 84; % of cals. from fat: 5; Fat: 0.5g; Sat. fat: trace; Carbs: 1g; Fiber: 0.5g; Sugars: 1g; Cholesterol: 47mg; Protein: 18g; Sodium: 35mg Vinaigrette: Cals.: 18; % of cals. from fat: 0; Fat: 0g; Sat. fat: 0g; Sodium: 438mg*

# grilled mexican chicken salad

This spicy chicken salad, made with corn, avocados, and chile peppers, is great as a main course or as part of a party buffet.

**SERVES 6**

2 WHOLE BONELESS, SKINLESS CHICKEN BREASTS
   (ABOUT 3 POUNDS), SPLIT
⅓ CUP FRESH LEMON JUICE
⅓ CUP PLUS 2 TABLESPOONS FRESH LIME JUICE
2 GARLIC CLOVES, THINLY SLICED
2 TEASPOONS GROUND CUMIN
½ CUP PLUS 2 TABLESPOONS OLIVE OIL
1 CUP HALVED CHERRY TOMATOES
1 CUP COOKED FRESH CORN KERNELS
   (FROM 2 EARS SWEET CORN)
3 SCALLIONS, TRIMMED AND MINCED
   (WHITE AND LIGHT GREEN PARTS)
1 TEASPOON FINELY MINCED FRESH GREEN CHILE PEPPER
1 RIPE AVOCADO
2 TABLESPOONS CHOPPED FRESH CILANTRO
KOSHER SALT AND FRESHLY GROUND BLACK PEPPER

**1.** Place the chicken in a large glass or ceramic baking dish. Combine the lemon juice, ⅓ cup of the lime juice, garlic, and cumin in a medium-size bowl. Slowly whisk in ½ cup of the oil. Pour the marinade over the chicken. Cover and refrigerate overnight, turning occasionally.

**2.** Prepare a charcoal or gas grill.

**3.** When the fire is medium-hot, and the coals are covered with a light coating of ash and glow deep red, lift the chicken from the marinade and grill 6 to 8 inches from the heat until nicely browned and the juices run clear when the chicken is pricked with a fork, about 10 to 15 minutes. Baste often with the marinade during grilling. (Alternatively, you may also cook the chicken under the broiler.)

**4.** When the chicken is cool enough to handle, cut the meat into pieces about 1½ inches long and place them in a large bowl.

5. Add the tomatoes, corn, scallions, and chile pepper to the chicken.

6. Peel, pit, and dice the avocado and add all but one-quarter to the salad.

7. To make the dressing, mash the remaining avocado in a small bowl and beat in the remaining lime juice until blended. Whisk in the remaining 2 tablespoons of the oil until well blended, then pour over the chicken salad. Add the cilantro and salt and pepper to taste and toss. Taste and adjust the seasonings. Serve at room temperature.

*• Nutritional content per serving: 6 servings per recipe: Cals.: 489; % of cals. from fat: 50; Fat: 27g; Sat. fat: 5g; Carbs: 12g; Fiber: 4g; Sugars: 2g; Cholesterol: 132mg; Protein: 50g; Sodium: 319mg*

# grilled steak & vegetable salad with sesame-ginger dressing

Here's a delicious main course salad that is very easy to put together for a quick weeknight dinner or an elegant weekend lunch. The Sesame-Ginger Dressing, which is also delicious over salad greens and Asian noodles, can be made up to 3 days ahead of time. Simply grill or broil the steak, blanch the vegetables, then assemble the salad.

**SERVES 6**

**SESAME-GINGER DRESSING:**
⅓ CUP LOW-SODIUM SOY SAUCE
¼ CUP WHITE VINEGAR
3 TABLESPOONS SESAME OIL
2-INCH PIECE FRESH GINGER, PEELED AND GRATED

1 FLANK OR SIRLOIN STEAK (ABOUT 2½ POUNDS)
1 POUND ASPARAGUS, TRIMMED AND CUT INTO 2-INCH PIECES
1 BUNCH BROCCOLI, CUT INTO BITE-SIZE FLORETS
3 SCALLIONS, TRIMMED AND MINCED
  (WHITE AND LIGHT GREEN PARTS), FOR GARNISH
2 TABLESPOONS SESAME SEEDS, FOR GARNISH

continued

1. To make the dressing, place the soy sauce, vinegar, sesame oil, and ginger in a blender and blend until well combined. Taste and adjust the seasonings. The dressing will keep, covered, in the refrigerator for up to 3 days.

2. Grill or broil the steak to desired doneness. Set aside to cool. Cut the steak into thin strips.

3. Bring a large pot of salted water to a rapid boil. Add the asparagus and blanch for 1 minute. Remove with tongs to a colander. Drain and let cool. Add the broccoli to the same water and blanch for 1 minute. Drain and let cool. Transfer to a large bowl.

4. Toss the vegetables with half of the dressing and transfer to a platter. Arrange the steak slices over the vegetables and drizzle with the remaining dressing. Garnish with the scallions and sesame seeds and serve warm or at room temperature.

• *Nutritional content per serving: 6 servings per recipe: Cals.: 219; % of cals. from fat: 5; Fat: 0.5g; Sat. fat: 6g; Carbs: 3g; Fiber: 1g; Sugars: 1g; Cholesterol: 88mg; Protein: 38g; Sodium: 142mg Vinaigrette: Cals.: 69; % of cals. from fat: 89; Fat: 7g; Sat. fat: 1g; Sodium: 343mg*

# Sunday Night
# Burgers & Salad Dinner

Grilled Turkey Burgers
with Red Onion Sauce
(page 101)

Asparagus & Celery Salad
with Walnut Dressing
(page 60)

Jicama, Orange, & Watercress Salad
(page 62)

Fresh Sliced Tomatoes

Honey Melon & Strawberries
with Lime-Yogurt Sauce
(page 227)

# greens

This is the golden age of greens—never have so many enjoyed a place on the American table. They show up in salads, sautéed side dishes, stews, and are braised along with meats and fish.

ARUGULA  A fiery, peppery green, also called rocket. It holds up to cooking and it can make any salad more interesting.

ENDIVE  A tight little head of crunchy, lightly bitter leaves. It can be used in salads, as a substitute for chips with dips, or braised or roasted to go along with hearty meat dishes.

BIBB AND BOSTON LETTUCES  Delicate loose leaves make these great in salads, often in combination with heartier greens such as romaine or even watercress.

CHICORY  Also called frisée and curly endive, it is a crisp bitter green that can be sautéed with lemon juice, olive oil, and garlic for a side dish or the pale inner leaves can be added to a salad.

LAMB'S TONGUE  Also called mache or corn salad, this most tender and often tiny of leaves makes a lovely addition to a salad, or it can be served on its own simply tossed with olive oil and a dash of lemon juice, salt, and pepper.

LEAF LETTUCES  Mild, mixable salad greens. These are best fresh, crisp and lightly dressed.

MUSTARD GREENS  There's a lot of zip to these greens. When tiny and tender they are great in salads, mixed with other milder lettuce; larger leaves can be cooked slowly as a side dish or added to soups and stews.

RADICCHIO  A lovely red-purple head of tightly closed, slightly bitter leaves. Radicchio is great in cold salads when combined with more tender greens. The whole or half heads braise nicely in a pan with roasts. Individual leaves can be sautéed just like spinach.

SWISS CHARD  It comes with red or white ribs and wide green leaves and is a member of the beet family. Steamed, stewed, or sautéed, it is packed with flavor and nutrition.

WATERCRESS  Another peppery green. Watercress is great in salads, sautéed as a side dish, or added to soups and sandwiches. It is also an excellent garnish.

chapter four **sandwiches, burgers, & wraps**

Sandwiches are the perfect party food for outdoor celebrations, casual weekend gatherings, lunch, or brunch. The challenge is to give them a party flavor by dishing up unexpected combinations and using the best ingredients and tastiest bread available. Consider recipes such as Avocado Salad, Black Bean, & Quinoa Wraps; White Bean Spread Sandwiches with Arugula & Tomatoes on baguettes; or Grilled Lamb & Cucumber Raita Pitas. And as a nod to those who love burgers (and who doesn't?), serve Grilled Turkey Burgers with Red Onion Sauce that rival the juiciest beef on a bun.

# tuna niçoise sandwiches

A good way to prepare these sandwiches is to scoop out the insides of the bread and fill them with tuna and layers of olives, tomato, egg, and salad greens, so you get more taste of salad than of bread.

**MAKES 6 SANDWICHES**

2 (6-OUNCE) CANS WATER-PACKED TUNA, WELL DRAINED
2 TABLESPOONS CHOPPED RED ONION
2 TABLESPOONS CHOPPED FRESH FLAT-LEAF PARSLEY
1 TABLESPOON DRAINED CAPERS
1 TEASPOON BALSAMIC OR RED WINE VINEGAR
1 TEASPOON FRESH LEMON JUICE
3 TABLESPOONS EXTRA-VIRGIN OLIVE OIL
FRESHLY GROUND BLACK PEPPER
1 LONG BAGUETTE, OR 3 (8-INCH) HERO ROLLS
12 KALAMATA OLIVES, PITTED AND HALVED
1 LARGE RIPE TOMATO, CUT INTO THIN SLICES AND HALVED
2 HARD-COOKED EGGS, PEELED AND THINLY SLICED
2 CUPS FRESH SALAD GREENS

1.  Put the tuna, onion, parsley, and capers in a large bowl and mix together with a fork until the tuna is flaky.

2.  Whisk together the vinegar, lemon juice, olive oil, and pepper to taste in a small bowl and pour over the tuna mixture. Toss well. Taste and adjust the seasonings, if necessary, and toss again.

3.  To assemble the sandwiches, using your hands or a spoon, hollow the top and bottom bread halves out to create a shell. Discard the insides. Fill the bottom half with the tuna salad. Top with the olive halves, tomato and egg slices, and salad greens. Drizzle with a bit of olive oil and pepper, if desired. Put the top pieces of the bread over the sandwiches and press down lightly on them. If using baguettes, cut into thirds crosswise. If using rolls, cut in half crosswise.

• *Nutritional content per serving: 6 servings per recipe: Cals.: 276; % of cals. from fat: 11; Fat: 11g; Sat. fat: 2g; Carbs: 35g; Fiber: 2g; Sugars: 2g; Cholesterol: 86mg; Protein: 19g; Sodium: 560mg*

**THE POWER COOK**

Even the simplest dish—turkey burgers, chicken thighs, Greek salad—can become a star if you take time to present the food beautifully.

Four simple tricks:

1. Dress the platter with red-edged lettuce leaves under the food.

2. Add chopped fresh herbs such as basil, parsley, or cilantro sprinkled lightly on top.

3. Indulge in the smallest touch of the exotic—topping with julienned roasted red pepper strips or pitted Moroccan olives.

4. Arrange food on an oversize platter around a condiment in a small dish—spiced ketchup for the burgers, for example, or a low-fat yogurt dill sauce for chicken or salad.

# white bean spread sandwiches with arugula & tomatoes

Canned white beans are a great pantry staple because they can be used in so many types of dishes. When blended with fresh basil, garlic, and olive oil, they make a delicious and versatile sandwich spread. It's also very good to serve with Crostini (page 22).

**MAKES 6 SANDWICHES**

2 (14- OR 15-OUNCE) CANS WHITE BEANS, RINSED AND DRAINED

¾ CUP PACKED FRESH BASIL LEAVES

2 GARLIC CLOVES, SLICED

3 TABLESPOONS EXTRA-VIRGIN OLIVE OIL

1 TEASPOON FRESH LEMON JUICE

KOSHER SALT AND FRESHLY GROUND BLACK PEPPER

2 LONG BAGUETTES, CUT IN HALF LENGTHWISE

2 CUPS ARUGULA LEAVES, RINSED AND COARSELY CHOPPED

2 MEDIUM TOMATOES, THINLY SLICED

1. Combine the beans, basil, and garlic in a food processor. Add the olive oil in a slow, steady stream with the motor running and pulse until very smooth. Add the lemon juice and salt and pepper to taste and pulse again. Taste and adjust the seasonings, if necessary. Refrigerate for at least 1 hour. (The spread can be made a day ahead of time and stored, covered, in the refrigerator. Bring to room temperature before serving.)

2. To assemble the sandwiches, cut the halved baguettes into 6-inch lengths. Spread 3 tablespoons of the bean mixture over each bottom half of the sandwich. Top with the arugula and tomato slices and remaining bread.

• *Nutritional content per serving: 6 servings per recipe: Cals.: 420; % of cals. from fat: 21; Fat: 10g; Sat. fat: 2g; Carbs: 67g; Fiber: 9g; Sugars: 4g; Cholesterol: 0mg; Protein: 16g; Sodium: 708mg*

# curried tuna & apple salad pitas

Light and tasty tuna salad tossed with a Granny Smith apple and chopped celery makes a perfect sandwich for a quick, healthy lunch for your family or weekend guests.

**MAKES 6 SANDWICHES**

2 (6-OUNCE) CANS WATER-PACKED TUNA, DRAINED
1 TABLESPOON FRESH LEMON JUICE
1/2 CUP CHOPPED CELERY
1/2 CUP CHOPPED UNPEELED GRANNY SMITH APPLE
3 TO 4 TABLESPOONS REDUCED-FAT MAYONNAISE
1 TEASPOON WHITE VINEGAR
1 TEASPOON CURRY POWDER
KOSHER SALT AND FRESHLY GROUND BLACK PEPPER
2 CUPS MIXED SALAD GREENS
6 PITAS, HALVED AND SPLIT

1. Put the tuna and the lemon juice in a large bowl and break up the tuna with a fork. Add the celery and apple and toss together.

2. In a small bowl whisk together the mayonnaise, vinegar, curry powder, and salt and pepper to taste. Mix the tuna mixture together with the mayonnaise until well combined. Taste and adjust the seasonings, if necessary.

3. Spoon the tuna salad and salad greens into each pita half. Keep refrigerated until serving.

• *Nutritional content per serving: 6 servings per recipe: Cals.: 256; % of cals. from fat: 10; Fat: 10g; Sat. fat: trace; Carbs: 38g; Fiber: 2g; Sugars: 5g; Cholesterol: 19mg; Protein: 19g; Sodium: 766mg*

# A Picnic Lunch
# in the Park

### Cool Cucumber, Yogurt, & Dill Soup
(page 33)

### White Bean Spread Sandwiches
### with Arugula & Tomatoes
(page 92)

### Curried Tuna & Apple Salad Pitas
(page 94)

### Sliced Watermelon

### Oatmeal Raisin Cookies
(page 208)

### Iced Mocha Cinnamon Coffee
(page 235)

# grilled lamb
# & cucumber raita pitas

Pitas stuffed with grilled lamb and tangy raita are delicious. Raita is a yogurt-based Indian dish, which can be considered a salad, side dish, or condiment. Its light and creamy coolness complements a variety of dishes.

**MAKES 12 SANDWICHES**

¼ CUP BALSAMIC VINEGAR

1 CUP DRY RED WINE

2 TABLESPOONS OLIVE OIL

3 LARGE GARLIC CLOVES, THINLY SLICED

1 TABLESPOON CRUSHED FRESH ROSEMARY, OR 1 TEASPOON DRIED

1 TEASPOON CHOPPED FRESH OREGANO OR, 1 TEASPOON DRIED

¼ CUP CHOPPED FRESH MINT

FRESHLY GROUND BLACK PEPPER

1 BUTTERFLIED LEG OF LAMB (3 TO 4 POUNDS)

**CUCUMBER RAITA:**

1 CUP LOW-FAT PLAIN YOGURT

1 TEASPOON GROUND CUMIN

PINCH OF CRUSHED RED PEPPER FLAKES

PINCH OF SUGAR

KOSHER SALT AND FRESHLY GROUND BLACK PEPPER

1 LARGE CUCUMBER OR 4 SMALL KIRBY CUCUMBERS,
   PEELED, SEEDED, AND DICED

¼ CUP FINELY DICED RED ONION

¼ CUP CHOPPED FRESH MINT

6 WHOLE WHEAT PITAS, 7 INCHES IN DIAMETER,
   SPLIT TO FORM POCKETS

3 CUPS FRESH SALAD GREENS

1½ CUPS CHOPPED FRESH TOMATO

1. In a medium bowl, whisk together the vinegar, wine, olive oil, garlic, rosemary, oregano, ¼ cup chopped mint, and pepper. Put the lamb in a large shallow nonreactive baking dish, pour the marinade over it, cover, and refrigerate for 2 to 6 hours, turning the lamb occasionally.

2. To make the raita, put the yogurt in a strainer lined with cheesecloth or a paper towel over a bowl. Drain for 15 minutes and transfer to a medium bowl. Add the cumin, red pepper flakes, sugar, and salt and pepper to taste and whisk together until creamy and well combined. Put the cucumbers, onion, and ¼ cup chopped mint in a large bowl and toss together. Pour the yogurt mixture over them and toss well to combine. Taste and adjust the seasonings. Cover and chill the raita for a few hours before serving.

3. Prepare a gas or charcoal grill or preheat the broiler. When the fire is medium-hot, and the coals are covered with a light coating of ash and glow deep red, lift the lamb from the marinade, and grill the lamb 4 to 6 inches from the fire for 15 to 20 minutes per side, turning occasionally. Or put the lamb in a broiler or roasting pan and put on a rack about 6 inches from the broiler. Broil for about 40 minutes, turning occasionally. After 30 minutes, check the lamb for doneness every few minutes. Do not overcook. Remove the lamb to a cutting board and let sit for 10 minutes.

4. Carve the lamb into thin slices. Fill each pita with the lamb, salad greens, and tomato, then spoon the raita into each pita. Serve at once.

• *Nutritional content per serving: 12 to 16 servings per recipe: Cals.: 210; % of cals. from fat: 30; Fat: 7g; Sat. fat: 2g; Carbs: 16g; Fiber: 1g; Sugars: 4g; Cholesterol: 52mg; Protein: 19g; Sodium: 189mg*

# chicken & cucumber salad pitas

This very light and creamy chicken salad is made with a dollop of mayonnaise and a generous amount of fat-free Greek yogurt, which has a fantastic taste and texture and is an excellent substitute in any type of mayonnaise-based salad. Greek yogurt is available in most supermarkets and health food stores.

**SERVES 6**

4 QUARTS WATER

2 CUPS 99% FAT-FREE LOW-SODIUM CHICKEN BROTH

1 ONION, PEELED

2 CARROTS, PEELED AND COARSELY CHOPPED

2 CELERY STALKS, COARSELY CHOPPED

4 BONELESS, SKINLESS CHICKEN BREAST HALVES
   (ABOUT 1½ POUNDS)

2 LARGE CUCUMBERS OR 4 SMALL KIRBY CUCUMBERS,
   PEELED, SEEDED, AND DICED

4 SCALLIONS, TRIMMED AND FINELY MINCED
   (WHITE AND LIGHT GREEN PARTS)

2 TABLESPOONS LOW-FAT MAYONNAISE

¾ CUP LOW-FAT GREEK YOGURT

1 TABLESPOON FRESH LEMON JUICE

KOSHER SALT AND FRESHLY GROUND BLACK PEPPER

6 PITAS

6 ROMAINE LETTUCE LEAVES

1. Put the water, broth, onion, carrots, and celery in a large soup pot and bring to a boil. Add the chicken to the broth and boil for 1 minute. Reduce the heat and simmer the chicken, partially covered, until the chicken is cooked through, 25 to 30 minutes. Remove the pot from the heat and let the chicken cool in the broth for 20 to 30 minutes.

2. Remove the chicken from the broth. Strain the broth and reserve for another use. Tear the chicken into bite-size pieces and put in a large bowl. Add the cucumbers and scallions to the chicken and toss well.

3. In a medium bowl, mix together the mayonnaise, yogurt, lemon juice, and salt and pepper to taste until smooth. Taste and adjust the seasonings, if necessary.

4. Gently fold the yogurt mixture into the chicken and gently toss until well combined. Cover and chill the salad if not serving right away.

5. Stuff each pita with the chicken salad and romaine lettuce and serve.

• *Nutritional content per serving: 6 servings per recipe: Cals.: 373; % of Cals. from fat: 10; Fat: 4g; Sat. fat: 1g; Carbs: 45g; Fiber: 4g; Sugars: 8g; Cholesterol: 76mg; Protein: 37g; Sodium: 75mg*

# Pool Party

### Strawberry-Mango Coolers
(page 229)

### Gazpacho with Grilled Shrimp & Corn
(page 34)

### Asian Turkey Salad Wraps
(page 103)

### Chicken & Cucumber Salad Pitas
(page 98)

### Honeydew Melon & Strawberries with Lime Yogurt Sauce
(page 227)

# grilled turkey burgers
# with red onion sauce

Grilled turkey burgers are as juicy and satisfying as burgers made with beef, but they are much lighter and lower in calories. The delectable Red Onion Sauce is great not only with grilled burgers, but also with grilled pork tenderloin, lamb chops, and vegetables.

**MAKES 6 BURGERS (ABOUT 2 CUPS)**

1¼ POUNDS GROUND TURKEY

⅔ CUP WHOLE WHEAT BREADCRUMBS

½ CUP FINELY CHOPPED ONION

⅓ CUP FINELY CHOPPED CELERY

1 LARGE EGG WHITE

½ TEASPOON DRIED THYME

½ TEASPOON CELERY SEEDS

KOSHER SALT AND FRESHLY GROUND BLACK PEPPER

**RED ONION SAUCE:**

4 LARGE RED ONIONS, CUT INTO ¼-INCH DICE

3 CUPS LOW-FAT LOW-SODIUM CHICKEN BROTH

¼ CUP DRY SHERRY

2 TABLESPOONS BALSAMIC VINEGAR

1 TEASPOON SUGAR

KOSHER SALT AND FRESHLY GROUND BLACK PEPPER TO TASTE

¾ CUP LOW-FAT PLAIN YOGURT

6 WHOLE WHEAT HAMBURGER BUNS

1. In a large mixing bowl, mix together the turkey, breadcrumbs, ½ cup chopped onion, celery, egg white, thyme, celery seeds, and salt and pepper to taste. Form into 6 patties, about ½ inch thick. Cover and refrigerate for up to 2 hours.

*continued*

2. To prepare the Red Onion Sauce, in a saucepan, mix together the diced red onions, broth, sherry, vinegar, and sugar. Bring to a boil over high heat. Reduce the heat and simmer, uncovered, stirring occasionally, until most of the liquid evaporates, 40 to 45 minutes. Season with salt and pepper to taste. Stir in the yogurt and cook over very low heat until the flavors blend, about 10 minutes longer. The sauce will keep, covered, in the refrigerator for up to a week. Serve warm or at room temperature.

3. Prepare a gas or charcoal grill. When the fire is medium-hot, and the coals are covered with a light coating of ash and glow deep red, grill the burgers, turning once, until browned on both sides and white, throughout, about 4 minutes per side. (Alternatively, you may also cook the burgers under the broiler.)

4. Serve the burgers on the rolls and spoon some of the Red Onion Sauce over each one.

• *Nutritional content per serving of single turkey burger: Cals.: 388; % of cals. from fat: 25; Fat: 4g; Sat. fat: 4g; Carbs: 46g; Fiber: 5g; Sugars: 13g; Cholesterol: 77mg; Protein: 26g; Sodium: 250mg*

# asian turkey salad wraps

Turkey should be cooked often, not just for the holidays, because the leftovers are so versatile and luscious. Here's a lightened-up twist on a turkey sandwich—shredded turkey and savoy cabbage with fresh herbs and Asian vinaigrette spooned into a wrap.

**MAKES 6 WRAPS**

3 CUPS SHREDDED TURKEY

2 CUPS SHREDDED SAVOY CABBAGE (SEE NOTE)

¼ CUP CHOPPED FRESH CILANTRO

2 TABLESPOONS CHOPPED FRESH MINT LEAVES

2 SCALLIONS, TRIMMED AND FINELY MINCED
   (WHITE AND LIGHT GREEN PARTS)

1 TABLESPOON DIJON MUSTARD

1 TABLESPOON RICE VINEGAR

2 TEASPOONS LOW-SODIUM SOY SAUCE

1 TEASPOON SESAME OIL

PINCH OF SUGAR

¼ CUP CORN OR CANOLA OIL

SIX FLOUR TORTILLAS OR WRAPS, 8 INCHES IN DIAMETER

1. Put the turkey, cabbage, cilantro, mint, and scallions in a large bowl. Toss together to mix well.

2. In a small bowl, whisk together the mustard, vinegar, soy sauce, sesame oil, and sugar. Slowly add the corn or canola oil, whisking constantly, until well combined.

3. Pour the vinaigrette over the turkey mixture and toss well to combine.

4. Spoon the turkey salad down the center of the wrap. Fold the sides toward the center of the wrap. Fold the bottom toward the center and roll toward the top. Cut the wrap on the diagonal and serve.

**Note:** You may use Chinese, green, or red cabbage, or any combination, in this recipe.

• *Nutritional content per serving: 6 servings per recipe: Cals.: 397; % of cals. from fat: 38; Fat: 17g; Sat. fat: 2g; Carbs: 26g; Fiber: 2g; Sugars: 2g; Cholesterol: 71mg; Protein: 35g; Sodium: 467mg*

# avocado salad, black bean, & quinoa wraps

These hearty Mexican-style wraps are good things to serve to a hungry crowd. Although they may seem a bit labor-intensive, they're really a snap to make, especially when the beans and grains are prepared ahead of time. The avocado salad can be put together right before assembling them. If using the canned bean option, the beans should always be well rinsed and drained before using to get rid of the salt that is added to them to help preserve their shape, texture, and flavor.

**MAKES 6 WRAPS**

3 RIPE AVOCADOS, PEELED, PITTED, AND COARSELY CHOPPED
2 LARGE TOMATOES, COARSELY CHOPPED
1 RED ONION, FINELY DICED
1 JALAPEÑO PEPPER, SEEDED AND FINELY CHOPPED
¼ CUP FINELY CHOPPED FRESH CILANTRO
¼ CUP EXTRA-VIRGIN OLIVE OIL
2 TABLESPOONS ORANGE JUICE
2 TABLESPOONS FRESH LIME JUICE
2 TABLESPOONS CHOPPED FRESH CILANTRO
1 TEASPOON GROUND CUMIN
¼ TEASPOON CHILI POWDER
KOSHER SALT AND FRESHLY GROUND BLACK PEPPER
SIX FLOUR TORTILLAS, 10 INCHES IN DIAMETER
2 CUPS COOKED BLACK BEANS OR 2 (15.5-OUNCE) CANS
   BLACK BEANS, WELL RINSED AND DRAINED
1½ CUPS COOKED QUINOA

1. In a large bowl, mix the avocados, tomatoes, onion, pepper, and ¼ cup chopped cilantro together until well combined.

2. In another bowl, whisk together the olive oil, orange juice, lime juice, 2 tablespoons chopped cilantro, cumin, chili powder, and salt and pepper to taste. Pour over the avocado mixture and toss gently to combine. Set aside.

**3.** To assemble the wraps, place a tortilla on a work surface and put a portion each of the black beans and quinoa in the center of it. Spoon the avocado mixture over it. Fold the sides in toward the center and roll firmly into a cylinder. Slice on the diagonal and serve.

• *Nutritional content per serving:6 servings per recipe: Cals.: 368; % of cals. from fat: 41; Fat: 31g; Sat. fat: 5g; Carbs: 86g; Fiber: 20g; Sugars: 7g; Cholesterol: 0mg; Protein: 19g; Sodium: 758mg*

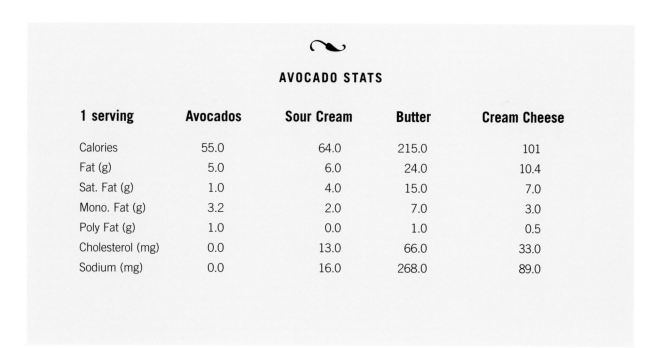

## AVOCADO STATS

| 1 serving | Avocados | Sour Cream | Butter | Cream Cheese |
|---|---|---|---|---|
| Calories | 55.0 | 64.0 | 215.0 | 101 |
| Fat (g) | 5.0 | 6.0 | 24.0 | 10.4 |
| Sat. Fat (g) | 1.0 | 4.0 | 15.0 | 7.0 |
| Mono. Fat (g) | 3.2 | 2.0 | 7.0 | 3.0 |
| Poly Fat (g) | 1.0 | 0.0 | 1.0 | 0.5 |
| Cholesterol (mg) | 0.0 | 13.0 | 66.0 | 33.0 |
| Sodium (mg) | 0.0 | 16.0 | 268.0 | 89.0 |

# Graduation Day Buffet

## Fresh Tomato Salsa
(page 14)

## Handmade Spicy Tortilla Chips
(page 12)

# Tuna Niçoise Sandwiches
(page 91)

# Avocado, Black Bean, & Quinoa Wraps
(page 104)

# Grilled Garlic Shrimp, White Bean, & Arugula Salad
(page 75)

# Tabbouleh & Vegetable Salad
(page 71)

# Caesar Salad
## with Lemon Vinaigrette & Water Chestnuts
(page 55)

# Chilled Minted Fruit
(page 228)

# Lemon Cookies
(page 207)

# fresh herbs

Herbs are the single best way to create a distinctively flavored dish without relying on fats and sugars for flavor. Whether dried or fresh, use them in everything from roast chicken to tomato sauce to sandwich spreads. To keep fresh herbs fresh, store in a plastic bag or container; some such as basil, which may come with its roots attached, can do well for a couple of days in a vase of water. Dried herbs should be in an airtight jar, out of the sunlight. Here's a look at some of the most useful and flavorful of the bunch.

BASIL  This Asian herb has been cultivated for more than 4,000 years because of its faintly minty and mildly peppery flavor. There are over 40 known varieties; sweet basil is most commonly used in cooking. It is a great addition to many Italian and Thai dishes and goes well with pasta and rice, as well as all types of meat, fish, and vegetables.

CHIVES  These little green spikes of oniony fire offer a lot of flavor when added to omelettes, cream and cheese sauces, soups, salad dressings, and sandwiches.

CILANTRO  This herb, and its seed called coriander, is one that people have extreme feelings about. For some its distinctively citrusy aroma and slightly jarring aftertaste just don't add up. We think it is wonderful.

DILL  A tiny bit goes a long way when using this feathery herb uncooked in creamy dips or in a salad; in cooked foods such as fish or chicken stews or soups you can be more generous.

PARSLEY  There are two basic types of parsley: curly leaf and Italian or flat leaf. The curly leaf is used mostly for a garnish; the flat leaf makes a good addition to fish, stews, and salads, and is a breath freshener. Crush parsley in your hand, tear it, or use a mortar and pestle before adding to food.

ROSEMARY  One or two small leaves crushed and added to a saucer of olive oil makes a dip for bread; a sprig or two of fresh leaves mixed with salt, pepper and minced garlic makes a dry rub for pork roasts and chicken. It is standard seasoning for roast lamb and is good in marinades.

SAGE  Once used as a medicinal tea, sage's delicately fried leaves make a superb garnish for chicken or fish. Fresh or dried, it offers an aromatic, minty-smokey flavor to stews, potatoes, and roasted vegetables. As part of a bouquet garni, it is used to flavor, stocks, soups, and broths.

chapter five **main courses**

D esigning a dinner party menu usually begins from the middle and works outward: First, you select an entrée, then decide on an accompanying appetizer, salad, side dish, and dessert. Just as you might match a wine to an entrée, you can build an entire meal that works together harmoniously—leading each guest on a culinary journey from the teasing tastes of the appetizers through the last act of dessert and coffee. Rethinking how to prepare party food— using the finest, freshest, purest ingredients and creating simple and often surprising flavors— leads naturally to new and healthy twists on old favorites.

# balsamic-glazed roasted chicken breasts

This versatile chicken dish pairs well with a variety of side dishes, including Sautéed Carrots with Black Olives (page 170) and Roasted Root Vegetables (page 182).

**SERVES 6**

6 BONE-IN CHICKEN BREASTS (ABOUT 5 POUNDS),
 TRIMMED, SKIN REMOVED
KOSHER SALT AND FRESHLY GROUND BLACK PEPPER
3 TEASPOONS DRIED THYME
⅓ CUP RED CURRANT JELLY
3 TABLESPOONS BALSAMIC VINEGAR
¼ CUP CHOPPED FRESH FLAT-LEAF PARSLEY, FOR GARNISH

1.  Preheat the oven to 400°F. Line a baking sheet with foil and lightly oil.

2.  Season the chicken on both sides with salt and pepper, then rub with 2½ teaspoons of the thyme. Place the chicken, bone side up, in a single layer on the prepared baking sheet. Roast in the oven for 20 minutes.

3.  Meanwhile, in a small saucepan, heat the jelly, vinegar, and the remaining ½ teaspoon of thyme over medium-low heat until the jelly is melted. Season to taste with additional salt and pepper and remove from the heat.

4.  Turn the chicken meat side up. Brush generously with the jelly glaze. Continue to roast, brushing with the remaining glaze, until the chicken is cooked through, about 20 minutes more. Garnish the chicken with parsley and serve at once.

• *Nutritional content per serving: 6 servings per recipe: Cals.: 338; % of cals. from fat: 18; Fat: 7g; Sat. fat: 2g; Carbs: 8g; Fiber: trace; Sugars: 6g; Cholesterol: 158mg; Protein: 58g; Sodium: 526mg*

# braised chicken & baby leeks

Try this dish of pure comfort food with Wild Rice & Toasted Almonds (page 191) and steamed haricots verts.

**SERVES 6**

3 POUNDS BONELESS, SKINLESS CHICKEN THIGHS
KOSHER SALT AND FRESHLY GROUND BLACK PEPPER
3 TABLESPOONS OLIVE OIL
6 SMALL LEEKS, HALVED, RINSED, AND DRAINED,
   CUT INTO 2-INCH PIECES
¾ CUP VEGETABLE BROTH
3 TABLESPOONS GRAINY MUSTARD
1 TABLESPOON BALSAMIC VINEGAR

1. Preheat the oven to 350°F.
2. Pat the chicken pieces dry and season with salt and pepper to taste. In a large skillet or sauté pan, heat 2 tablespoons of the olive oil and cook the chicken over medium heat until lightly browned, about 3 minutes per side. Remove the chicken with a slotted spoon to a bowl. Pour off all of the oil and wipe the pan clean with paper towels.
3. Heat the remaining tablespoon of olive oil in the pan and add the leeks. Cook over medium heat, stirring, until coated, about 1 minute. Add ½ cup of the broth, bring to a boil, reduce the heat, and simmer until the leeks are just tender, 5 to 7 minutes.
4. In a small bowl, mix the mustard and vinegar together.
5. Spoon the leeks into a 9 x 13–inch baking dish to cover the bottom and add a bit more broth. Put the chicken over the leeks and brush each thigh with the mustard mixture. Bake the chicken, basting occasionally, until the chicken is cooked through and juices run clear, about 50 minutes.

• *Nutritional content per serving: 6 servings per recipe: Cals.: 394; % of cals. from fat: 54; Fat: 24g; Sat. fat: 6g; Carbs: 3g; Fiber: trace; Sugars: 1g; Cholesterol: 145mg; Protein: 40g; Sodium: 535mg*

# grilled chicken kabobs
# with peach salsa

Serve these grilled chicken kabobs with a tangy peach salsa on the side.
The salsa is also an excellent accompaniment to barbecued beef or pork.

**SERVES 6; MAKES 1½ CUPS SALSA**

**CHICKEN:**
¾ CUP OLIVE OIL
¼ CUP FRESH LEMON JUICE
8 GARLIC CLOVES, PEELED AND HALVED
1 TABLESPOON HERBES DE PROVENCE
KOSHER SALT AND FRESHLY GROUND BLACK PEPPER
3 WHOLE BONELESS, SKINLESS CHICKEN BREASTS,
   RINSED AND PATTED DRY, CUT INTO ½-INCH CUBES

**PEACH SALSA:**
1 TABLESPOON OLIVE OIL
12 GARLIC CLOVES, THINLY SLICED
8 SHALLOTS, PEELED AND THINLY SLICED
1 CUP DRY WHITE WINE
4 LARGE PEACHES, PEELED, PITTED,
   AND CUT INTO ½-INCH WEDGES
2 PLUM TOMATOES, CUT INTO ½-INCH WEDGES
1 TABLESPOON LOW-SODIUM SOY SAUCE
¼ CUP DARK BROWN SUGAR
½ TEASPOON RED PEPPER FLAKES

   1. To prepare the chicken, combine the ¾ cup olive oil, lemon juice, 8
halved garlic cloves, herbes de Provence, and salt and pepper to taste in a
large glass or ceramic bowl. Add the chicken pieces, toss well, cover, and
marinate in the refrigerator for 6 to 8 hours.

   2. To prepare the salsa, heat the 1 tablespoon olive oil in a large sauté
pan over medium heat. Cook the 12 sliced garlic cloves and shallots,
stirring, until softened and golden, about 10 minutes. Add the wine, bring
to a boil, then simmer, uncovered, for 15 minutes.

**3.** Add the peaches, tomatoes, soy sauce, brown sugar, and red pepper flakes to the pan and bring to a boil over high heat. Reduce the heat to medium and cook, stirring frequently, for 20 minutes. The peaches and tomatoes should be broken down but remain fairly chunky. Taste and adjust the seasonings. Let cool and refrigerate until ready to serve. The salsa can be made up to 3 days ahead of time.

**4.** Prepare a gas or charcoal grill. Thread 6 skewers with the marinated chicken squares. When the fire is medium-hot, and the coals are covered with a light coating of ash and glow deep red, grill the kabobs 5 or 6 inches over the coals, turning them once or twice, until cooked through, 10 to 15 minutes.

**5.** Serve the kabobs with a few tablespoons of peach salsa on the side.

• *Nutritional content per serving: 6 servings per recipe: Chicken: Cals.: 120; % cals. from fat: 20%; Fat: 4g; Sat fat: 0g; Carbs: 0g; Fiber: 0g; Sugars: 23g; Cholesterol: 55mg; Protein: 0g; Sodium: 55mg Salsa: 6 servings per recipe: Cals.: 100; % of cals. from fat: 42%; Fat: 2g; Sat. fat: 0g; Carbs: 2g; Fiber: 13g; Sugars: 1g; Cholesterol: 75mg; Protein: 0g; Sodium: 17g*

# grilled jerk chicken

Skinned and boneless chicken thighs are great for cooking on the grill because they stay moist and flavorful. They are especially good in this version of jerk chicken. If you like your chicken spicy, add another jalapeño pepper and more hot sauce to the marinade.

**SERVES 6**

1 RED ONION, COARSELY CHOPPED
4 GARLIC CLOVES, CHOPPED
1 JALAPEÑO PEPPER, SEEDED AND MINCED
1 TABLESPOON LIGHT BROWN SUGAR
2 TEASPOONS FIVE-SPICE POWDER
¼ CUP RICE WINE VINEGAR
2 TABLESPOONS LOW-SODIUM SOY SAUCE
2 TEASPOONS HOT SAUCE
3 POUNDS BONELESS, SKINLESS CHICKEN THIGHS

1. Put the onion, garlic, pepper, sugar, five-spice powder, vinegar, soy sauce, and hot sauce in a blender and blend until very smooth.

2. Put the chicken in a large bowl. Pour the marinade over it and toss well to coat. Cover and let marinate in the refrigerator for up to 8 hours or overnight.

3. Prepare a gas or charcoal grill. When the fire is medium–hot, and the coals are covered with a light coating of ash and glow deep red, grill the chicken, turning often and basting with the marinade, until cooked through, about 20 minutes. Serve at once.

• *Nutritional content per serving: 6 servings per recipe: Cals.: 192; % of cals. from fat: 25; Fat: 5g; Sat. fat: 1g; Carbs: 7g; Fiber: trace; Sugars: 5g; Cholesterol: 114mg; Protein: 28g; Sodium: 312mg*

# roasted cornish game hens with citrus sauce

Cornish hens are a good alternative to roast chicken. In this recipe they are bathed and roasted in a marinade of fresh lime and orange juices, soy sauce, and grapeseed oil. These are also delicious cooked on the grill.

**SERVES 6**

3 CORNISH GAME HENS (6½ TO 7½ POUNDS), SPLIT
½ CUP FRESH LIME JUICE (FROM 2 LIMES)
1 TABLESPOON FRESH ORANGE JUICE
1 TABLESPOON LOW-SODIUM SOY SAUCE
1 TABLESPOON GRAPESEED OIL
2 BUNCHES WATERCRESS, STEMMED
LIME WEDGES, FOR GARNISH

1. Preheat the oven to 350°F.

2. Put the game hens in a large roasting pan lined with foil. In a small bowl, whisk together the lime juice, orange juice, soy sauce, and oil. Pour over the game hens and baste.

3. Roast the hens for 1½ hours, basting frequently with the lime marinade.

4. To serve, arrange the watercress on a large platter. Put the hens on the watercress and drizzle with any remaining marinade, if desired. Garnish with lime wedges and serve at once.

• *Nutritional content per serving: 6 servings per recipe: Cals.: 317; % of cals. from fat: 30; Fat: 10g; Sat. fat: 2g; Carbs: 4g; Fiber: trace; Sugars: 3g; Cholesterol: 221mg; Protein: 50g; Sodium: 209mg*

# turkey or chicken scallopini with white wine sauce

Scallopini, made with either turkey or chicken cutlets, is a quick and delicious dish to prepare for an elegant dinner party. It's fabulous with brown or wild rice.

**SERVES 6**

3 TABLESPOONS INSTANT OR UNBLEACHED
   ALL-PURPOSE FLOUR (SEE NOTE)
1½ TO 2 POUNDS TURKEY OR CHICKEN SCALLOPINI
   (ABOUT 12 PIECES)
KOSHER SALT AND FRESHLY GROUND BLACK PEPPER
3 TABLESPOONS OLIVE OIL
3 GARLIC CLOVES, THINLY SLICED
2 TEASPOONS CHOPPED FRESH SAGE OR 1 TEASPOON DRIED
½ CUP DRY WHITE WINE
1 CUP 99% FAT-FREE CHICKEN BROTH
1 TEASPOON FRESH LEMON JUICE
1 TEASPOON BUTTER
½ CUP CHOPPED FRESH FLAT-LEAF PARSLEY, FOR GARNISH

1.  Spread the flour on a large plate. Pat the cutlets dry with paper towels and season with salt and pepper to taste. Dredge lightly with flour, shaking off any excess.

2.  In a large nonstick skillet, heat 1 tablespoon of the oil over medium-high heat. Add one-third of the cutlets and cook until golden outside and no longer pink inside, 1 to 2 minutes per side. Transfer to a platter and keep in a warm oven. Cook the remaining cutlets in another 1 tablespoon of the oil and transfer to the warm platter.

3.  Add the remaining tablespoon of oil to the pan. Add the garlic and sage and cook, stirring, until fragrant, about 1 minute. Add the wine, stirring and scraping up any browned bits, until reduced by half, about 2 minutes. Add the broth and cook, stirring, until reduced by half, 4 to 5 minutes. Add the lemon juice, stir, and remove from the heat. Whisk in the butter and taste and adjust the seasonings, if necessary

**4.** Spoon the sauce over the warm cutlets, garnish with parsley, and serve at once.

**Note:** Instant flour, such as Wondra®, makes a very light and crisp crust for sautéed fillets of poultry, meat, or fish.

• *Nutritional content per serving: 6 servings per recipe: Cals.: 205; % of cals. from fat: 38; Fat: 19g; Sat. fat: 2g; Carbs: 4g; Fiber: trace; Sugars: 1g; Cholesterol: 57mg; Protein: 23g; Sodium: 428mg*

## SASSY SEASONINGS

There are a number of good spices and spice blends that can add zest and flavor to your cooking. Most of these can be found in health food stores, Asian and Indian markets, and the international sections of some supermarkets. All spices should be stored in a cool, dry place for no longer then 6 months. A few examples are:

### Garam Masala

A blend of dry-roasted, ground spices used in Indian cooking. There are many variations of garam masala. It may contain up to 12 spices, such as black pepper, cinnamon, cloves, coriander, cumin, cardamom, dried chiles, fennel, mace, and nutmeg. Garam masala, which is excellent with meat, fish, and rice dishes, is usually added to a dish at the end of cooking or just before serving it.

### Fenugreek

An aromatic plant known for its pleasantly bitter, slightly sweet seeds. Fenugreek seeds, which come whole or ground, are used to flavor curry powders and spice blends. It is very good when sprinkled over salads and steamed or grilled vegetables.

### Herbes de Provence

A mixture of dried herbs, which most commonly contains basil, fennel seeds, lavender, marjoram, rosemary, sage, and thyme. The blend can be used in meat, poultry, and vegetable dishes as well as in sauces, soups, and stews.

### Sambal Oelek

A multipurpose condiment that is a paste of hot chile peppers, various spices, and lime juice. It is used as a condiment in Indian and Asian dishes and is very hot and spicy. It is also very good when added to soups, stews, and rice dishes.

# holiday roast turkey
# with rice & spinach stuffing

Serving savory golden roast turkey is a time-honored holiday tradition
in most homes. This recipe for lightened-up roast turkey with rice and
spinach stuffing is sure to please all of your dinner guests. The stuffing
can be made up to 2 days ahead of time—which is of great help
to the cook—and can be stuffed and cooked inside the bird or warmed
separately in the oven. Either way, it's light and delicious.

**SERVES 12, PLUS LEFTOVERS**

**ROAST TURKEY:**
1 TURKEY WITH GIBLETS (12 TO 14 POUNDS)
KOSHER SALT AND FRESHLY GROUND BLACK PEPPER
RICE & SPINACH STUFFING (RECIPE FOLLOWS)
¼ CUP WHITE WINE OR 99% FAT-FREE CHICKEN BROTH,
  FOR BASTING

**SHERRY GRAVY:**
2 TEASPOONS OLIVE OIL
2 CARROTS, PEELED AND CHOPPED
2 ONIONS, CHOPPED
2 STALKS CELERY, CHOPPED
3 GARLIC CLOVES, UNPEELED
4 CUPS 99% FAT-FREE CHICKEN BROTH
4 SPRIGS FRESH THYME OR 1 TEASPOON DRIED
FRESHLY GROUND BLACK PEPPER
¾ CUP DRY SHERRY
1 TEASPOON BALSAMIC VINEGAR
1 TEASPOON WORCESTERSHIRE SAUCE
3 TABLESPOONS WATER
2 TABLESPOONS CORNSTARCH
KOSHER SALT

1. Position an oven rack to the lower third of the oven; preheat to 425°F.

2. Put a roasting rack in a large roasting pan and put the turkey on it. Remove the giblets and neck from the turkey and reserve for stock (discard liver). Rinse inside and out with cold water and pat dry. Season the cavity with salt and pepper to taste. If roasting the turkey stuffed, loosely fill the cavity with stuffing and truss with trussing skewers and kitchen twine to close the cavity. Put remaining stuffing in baking dish and set aside. Tie the drumsticks together with twine and tuck the wing tips behind back.

3. Roast the turkey for 20 minutes. Reduce the temperature to 325°F and continue roasting, basting occasionally with the wine or broth, until an instant-read thermometer inserted in the thickest part of the thigh reads 180°F, about 3 hours. (If the turkey is browning too quickly, tent it loosely with foil.)

4. Meanwhile, to make the gravy, in a large heavy saucepan, heat the oil over medium heat. Add the carrots, onions, celery, garlic, and reserved giblets and neck, and cook, stirring occasionally, until well browned, about 20 minutes. Add the 4 cups broth, thyme, and pepper. Bring to a boil, reduce heat to low and simmer, partially covered, for 30 minutes. Let cool and strain through a fine sieve. Chill until ready to use. Skim off fat before cooking.

5. When the turkey is done, transfer it to a carving board, tent loosely with foil, and let it rest for 20 to 30 minutes.

6. Strain the drippings from the roasting pan into a bowl and chill in the freezer for 20 minutes. Put the roasting pan over 2 burners on the stove, add the sherry, and cook over medium-low heat, stirring and scraping up any browned bits, for about 1 minute. Strain into a saucepan. Add the reserved giblet stock and bring to a simmer. Skim and discard the fat from the chilled pan juices and add to the simmering stock. Stir in the vinegar and Worcestershire sauce.

7. In a small bowl, combine the water and cornstarch. Slowly add to the simmering gravy, whisking until slightly thickened. Season to taste with salt and pepper.

8. Remove the twine from the turkey. Scoop out the stuffing and transfer to a serving bowl, if necessary. Carve the turkey, discarding the skin. Serve with the gravy.

• *Nutritional content per serving: 16 servings per recipe: Cals.: 563; % of cals. from fat: 12; Fat: 7g; Sat. fat: 2g; Carbs: 24g; Fiber: trace; Sugars: 3g; Cholesterol: 149mg; Protein: 51g; Sodium: 598mg*

# rice & spinach stuffing

**MAKES ABOUT 10 CUPS, OR 12 SERVINGS**

2 CUPS LONG-GRAIN RICE

3¾ CUPS 99% FAT-FREE CHICKEN BROTH

⅓ CUP MADEIRA WINE

1 TEASPOON DRIED SAGE

1 TEASPOON DRIED THYME

1 TABLESPOON CANOLA OIL

3 LEEKS (WHITE AND LIGHT GREEN PARTS)
   RINSED, DRAINED, AND CHOPPED

1 ONION, CHOPPED

2 STALKS CELERY, CHOPPED

½ CUP CHOPPED SHIITAKE MUSHROOMS

3 GARLIC CLOVES, THINLY SLICED

2 CUPS FRESH SPINACH LEAVES, RINSED AND COARSELY CHOPPED

KOSHER SALT AND FRESHLY GROUND BLACK PEPPER

1. Preheat the oven to 450°F.

2. Put the rice in a 9 x 13–inch baking dish. In a saucepan, combine the broth, wine, sage, and thyme. Bring to a boil and pour over the rice. Cover tightly with foil and bake until the rice is tender, about 30 minutes.

3. Meanwhile, in a large skillet or sauté pan, heat the oil over medium heat. Add the leeks, onion, and celery and cook, stirring occasionally, until tender, 8 to 10 minutes.

4. Add the mushrooms and garlic and cook, stirring, until mushrooms are lightly browned, about 5 minutes. Add the spinach and cook, stirring, until the spinach is just wilted, about 2 minutes. Stir into the rice. Season with salt and pepper to taste. The stuffing will keep, covered, in the refrigerator, for up to 2 days.

5. If serving the stuffing separately, cover and keep warm in a 250°F oven for up to an hour. If serving stuffed inside the turkey, let cool to room temperature before stuffing. If preparing stuffing ahead of time, keep covered in the refrigerator, and reheat, covered, in a 250°F oven for an hour.

• *Nutritional content per serving: 12 servings per recipe: Cals.: 66; % of cals. from fat: 19; Fat: 1g; Sat. fat: 0g; Carbs: 11g; Fiber: 1g; Sugars: 2g; Cholesterol: 1mg; Protein: 2g; Sodium: 417mg*

**RICE**

Raw rice will not cook very well inside a turkey, which is why the stuffing needs to be cooked and cooled before stuffing into a turkey.

# veal stew with tomatoes, peas, & mushrooms

This is an elegant and delicious dish that works well for almost any type of dinner party. When making this savory stew, be sure to buy top-quality veal.

**SERVES 6 TO 8**

3 TABLESPOONS OLIVE OIL

¼ CUP CHOPPED SHALLOTS

3 POUNDS BONELESS VEAL, TRIMMED AND CUT INTO 1½-INCH CUBES

KOSHER SALT AND FRESHLY GROUND BLACK PEPPER

2 (28-OUNCE) CANS PLUM TOMATOES WITH THEIR JUICE,
    COARSELY CHOPPED

½ CUP STEMMED AND THINLY SLICED CREMINI MUSHROOMS

½ CUP STEMMED AND THINLY SLICED SHIITAKE MUSHROOMS

1 (10-OUNCE) PACKAGE FROZEN PEAS, THAWED

½ CUP CHOPPED FRESH FLAT-LEAF PARSLEY, FOR GARNISH

1. In a large soup pot or Dutch oven, heat 2 tablespoons of the olive oil over medium heat. Add the shallots and cook, stirring, until golden, about 5 minutes.

2. Pat the veal pieces dry and add to the pot, browning them well on all sides. This may have to be done in batches.

3. Return all of the meat to the pot. Add salt and pepper to taste and the tomatoes. Bring to a boil and reduce the heat to a very low simmer. Cook the stew, partially covered and stirring occasionally, until the veal is very tender, about 1½ hours. (The stew can be prepared ahead of time up to this point. Cool, cover, and refrigerate for up to 2 days. Bring to room temperature before reheating.)

4. About 20 minutes before serving, heat the remaining tablespoon of oil in a skillet. Add the mushrooms and cook, stirring, until nicely browned, about 10 minutes. Stir them into the stew. Add the peas to the stew about 5 minutes before serving the stew. Taste and adjust the seasonings.

5. Serve the stew in shallow bowls garnished with parsley.

• *Nutritional content per serving: 6 to 8 servings per recipe: Cals.: 425; % of cals. from fat: 29; Fat: 14g; Sat. fat: 3g; Carbs: 23g; Fiber: 6g; Sugars: 10g; Cholesterol: 180mg; Protein: 54g; Sodium: 714mg*

# mushrooms

There are over 2,500 mushroom varieties grown in the world today. More and more of these delicious denizens of the damp are turning up in a variety of dishes. If you choose wild mushrooms, be certain of their source and safety. To clean fresh mushrooms, it is best to brush them and pick off any dirt, unless they are very dirty. If washing is required, do so immediately before use.

WHITE  These smooth, round, button-topped mushrooms are mild, although their flavor intensifies when they are cooked. They are served stuffed for appetizers, as additions to entrées, as sautéed sides, or grilled, sautéed, or braised as an addition to soups, stews, and casseroles.

CREMINI  Cremini mushrooms are a darker brown than their cousins, the white mushrooms. They also have a denser flavor and texture and add more zip to cooked foods.

PORTOBELLO  The portobello is simply a grown up cremini. With a cap up to 6 inches in diameter, they can be grilled whole, oven roasted, sliced, and sautéed, Select ones that are not shriveled or glossy and damp.

OYSTER  With their velvety texture and mild flavor, these fluted mushrooms are best sautéed with butter and onions and added to chicken, veal, pork, or seafood dishes.

SHIITAKE  Another mushroom made for cooking, not eating raw, the shiitake has an umbrella-like cap and a soft, spongy texture. Tear off the stems and set aside for use in stocks. When cooked they have a woodsy aroma. Best in stir-frys, pastas, and soups or prepared as a side dish.

ENOKI  The long slender stems of the enoki, topped with tiny caps, look like some underwater sea creature. Trim off roots before using and separate stems. Their mild, light flavor complements many dishes and they can be used as a garnish in soups and salads.

MOREL  A wild mushroom with a honeycombed pointed cap, a morel may be tan, yellow, or black. It has a nutty, rich flavor and woodsy aroma. It is useful in most styles of cooking and can be stuffed, sautéed, stewed, or added to casseroles, many French dishes, and soups.

PORCINI OR CEPES  These are also wild mushrooms, and are available fresh in limited quantities; always inspect and clean well and choose only young small ones. They have full caps and wide short stems and when cooked are creamy and nutty, with a meaty texture. Dried are available year-round. Ideal for soups, sauces, risotto, polenta, and pasta.

# savory beef & vegetable stew

Simmering beef and vegetable stew is an excellent dish to serve for a casual dinner party. Use hot Spanish or Hungarian paprika and cumin in this dish, which adds a delicious, pungent flavor to the stew.

**SERVES 6**

3 TABLESPOONS OLIVE OIL
2 POUNDS TOP ROUND OF BEEF, WELL TRIMMED,
   CUT INTO 1-INCH PIECES
KOSHER SALT AND FRESHLY GROUND BLACK PEPPER
1 ONION, CHOPPED
3 GARLIC CLOVES, THINLY SLICED
1 CARROT, CHOPPED
1 TABLESPOON HOT PAPRIKA
2 TEASPOONS GROUND CUMIN
3 CUPS LOW-FAT BEEF BROTH
1 CUP DRY RED WINE
1 CUP PLUM TOMATOES WITH JUICE, COARSELY CHOPPED
1 TABLESPOON CHOPPED FRESH THYME OR 1 TEASPOON DRIED
1 BAY LEAF
4 CARROTS, PEELED AND CUT INTO ¼-INCH DIAGONAL SLICES
12 SHALLOTS, PEELED
1 CUP SLICED WHITE OR CREMINI MUSHROOMS
½ CUP SLICED SHIITAKE MUSHROOMS
½ CUP CHOPPED FRESH FLAT-LEAF PARSLEY
12 FINGERLING OR SMALL RED POTATOES, HALVED

1.  In a large soup pot or Dutch oven, heat 2 tablespoons of the oil. Add the beef, season with salt and pepper to taste, and cook over medium-high heat, until browned an all sides, about 5 minutes. This may have to be done in batches. Remove the beef with a slotted spoon, leaving the drippings in the pan.

2.  Add the onion, garlic, and chopped carrot to the pot and cook, stirring frequently, until softened, about 8 minutes. Return the meat and any accumulated juices to the pan. Add the paprika and cumin and stir well to combine.

**3.** Add the broth, wine, tomatoes, thyme, and bay leaf. Bring to a boil, reduce the heat to low and simmer, covered, until the meat is tender, 1½ hours. Skim off any fat that has accumulated on the surface. (The stew can be prepared up to this point and refrigerated for up to 2 days. Reheat before proceding.)

**4.** Add the 4 sliced carrots and shallots and simmer, uncovered, over medium heat, until the vegetables are tender, about 30 minutes.

**5.** Meanwhile, heat the remaining tablespoon of olive oil in a large skillet. Add the mushrooms and cook over medium-high heat, stirring frequently, until softened and browned, about 5 minutes. Add the mushrooms and parsley to the stew about 5 minutes before the vegetables are done.

**6.** Also while the stew is cooking, place the potatoes in a vegetable steamer in a pot over simmering water and steam until fork-tender, about 15 minutes.

**7.** Serve the stew at once in large shallow bowls spooned over the potatoes.

• *Nutritional content per serving: 6 servings per recipe: Cals.: 496; % of cals. from fat: 29; Fat: 16g; Sat. fat: 4g; Carbs: 42g; Fiber: 7g; Sugars: 10g; Cholesterol: 91mg; Protein: 40g; Sodium: 950mg*

# beef, red pepper, & chinese cabbage stir-fry

Stir-fries work well for people who are watching their intake of fat and calories because meat can be used in smaller portions and play a supporting role in the dish. Try this delicious stir-fry where beef complements the tastes of red peppers, scallions, and Chinese cabbage.

**SERVES 6**

1 TEASPOON CORNSTARCH

1 CUP LOW-FAT BEEF BROTH

2 TABLESPOONS LOW-SODIUM SOY SAUCE

2 TABLESPOONS DRY SHERRY

½ TEASPOON TOASTED SESAME OIL

PINCH OF DRIED RED PEPPER FLAKES

3 TABLESPOONS SESAME SEEDS

1 POUND LEAN BEEF ROUND OR SIRLOIN,
    WELL TRIMMED AND CUT INTO THIN STRIPS

FRESHLY GROUND BLACK PEPPER

2 TEASPOONS VEGETABLE OIL

2 RED BELL PEPPERS, SEEDED, DEVEINED, AND THINLY SLICED

6 SCALLIONS, TRIMMED AND CUT DIAGONALLY
    INTO 1-INCH PIECES (WHITE AND LIGHT GREEN PARTS)

1 GARLIC CLOVE, FINELY MINCED

1 TABLESPOON FINELY MINCED GINGER

3 CUPS FINELY SHREDDED CHINESE CABBAGE

BROWN RICE, FOR SERVING (OPTIONAL)

1. In a small bowl, whisk together the cornstarch, broth, soy sauce, sherry, sesame oil, and pepper flakes. Set aside.

2. Toast the sesame seeds in a small skillet over medium heat, stirring occasionally, until golden and fragrant, about 5 minutes. Set aside.

3. Season the beef with the pepper to taste. Heat 1 teaspoon of the oil in a large skillet or wok over high heat. Add the beef and stir-fry until the meat is seared, 2 to 3 minutes. Remove with a slotted spoon and set aside.

continued

**4.** Add the remaining teaspoon of the oil to the pan. Add the peppers and stir-fry over medium-high heat until crisp-tender, about 3 minutes. Add the scallions, garlic, and ginger and cook, stirring, for 2 minutes. Add the cabbage and cook, stirring, for 1 minute.

**5.** Reduce the heat to medium and stir the sauce mixture into the pan. Cook, stirring constantly, until the sauce comes to a boil and thickens, about 3 minutes. Stir in the beef and juices and heat through.

**6.** Spoon the stir-fry over brown rice, if desired, sprinkle with the sesame seeds, and serve at once.

• *Nutritional content per serving: 6 servings per recipe: Cals.: 162; % of cals. from fat: 36; Fat: 6g; Sat. fat: 2g; Carbs: 6g; Fiber: 27g; Sugars: 13g; Cholesterol: 45mg; Protein: 19g; Sodium: 381mg*

# grilled lamb chops
# with tarragon-mustard sauce

Tangy mustard sauce laced with fresh tarragon is a delicious accompaniment to succulent lamb chops cooked on the grill. These are very good with Warm Lentils & Sautéed Spinach (page 183).

**SERVES 6**

**TARRAGON-MUSTARD SAUCE:**
⅓ CUP DIJON MUSTARD
2 TABLESPOONS RICE WINE VINEGAR
2 TABLESPOONS CHOPPED FRESH TARRAGON LEAVES
FRESHLY GROUND BLACK PEPPER

**CHOPS:**
12 LOIN OR RIB LAMB CHOPS, EACH ABOUT 2 INCHES THICK
FRESHLY GROUND BLACK PEPPER

1. To make the Tarragon-Mustard Sauce, in a bowl, stir together the mustard, vinegar, tarragon, and pepper to taste.
2. To grill the chops, generously season the chops with pepper to taste.
3. Prepare a gas or charcoal grill. Spray the grill rack with cooking spray.
4. When the fire is medium-hot, and the coals are covered with a light coating of ash and glow deep red, grill the chops for 5 to 6 minutes on each side until medium-rare, or cooked to desired degree of doneness, when an instant-read thermometer registers 140°F for rare, 150°F for medium, or 160°F for well-done meat. Season with a little more pepper just before serving, if desired. Pass the mustard sauce on the side.

*• Nutritional content per serving: 6 servings per recipe: Cals.: 420; % of cals. from fat: 40; Fat: 19g; Sat. fat: 7g; Carbs: 0g; Fiber: 0g; Sugars: 0g; Cholesterol: 183mg; Protein: 58g; Sodium: 162mg*

# grilled lamb kabobs
# with yogurt-mint sauce

Grilled lamb marinated in olive oil and balsamic vinegar tastes wonderful
with cool and refreshing Yogurt–Mint Sauce. I always make a generous
amount of this sauce and use the extra to spoon over juicy ripe tomatoes
or mix into tuna or chicken salad.

**SERVES 6; MAKES ABOUT 2 CUPS SAUCE**

**YOGURT-MINT SAUCE:**
2 CUPS PLAIN LOW-FAT YOGURT
½ CUP CHOPPED FRESH MINT LEAVES
¼ CUP CHOPPED FRESH FLAT-LEAF PARSLEY
1 TABLESPOON FRESH LEMON JUICE
KOSHER SALT AND FRESHLY GROUND BLACK PEPPER

**LAMB:**
3 TABLESPOONS OLIVE OIL
1 TABLESPOON BALSAMIC VINEGAR
1 TABLESPOON CHOPPED FRESH THYME OR 1 TEASPOON DRIED
2 GARLIC CLOVES, THINLY SLICED
2½ TO 3 POUNDS BONELESS LAMB,
   TRIMMED AND CUT INTO 2-INCH CUBES
KOSHER SALT AND FRESHLY GROUND BLACK PEPPER

**1.** To prepare the Yogurt–Mint Sauce, stir the yogurt, mint, parsley, lemon
juice, and salt and pepper to taste together until well blended. Refrigerate,
covered, until ready to serve.

**2.** To prepare the lamb, in a small bowl, whisk together the olive oil,
vinegar, thyme, and garlic.

**3.** Put the lamb cubes in a large nonreactive bowl and pour the
marinade over them. Add salt and pepper to taste and toss together to mix
well. Let the lamb marinate, at room temperature, for an hour. Thread the
lamb onto metal skewers, about 5 or 6 pieces per skewer, and baste with
the remaining marinade.

*continued*

**4.** Prepare a gas or charcoal grill. Spray the grill rack with cooking spray. When the fire is medium-hot, and the coals are covered with a light coating of ash and glow deep red, cook the lamb, with the grill covered, until lightly browned, about 5 minutes per side for medium-rare, or until desired doneness.

• *Nutritional content per serving: 6 servings per recipe: Cals.: 404; % of cals. from fat: 44; Fat: 20g; Sat. fat: 6g; Carbs: 8g; Fiber: 0g; Sugars: 5g; Cholesterol: 138mg; Protein: 46g; Sodium: 590mg*

# grilled pork chops
# & portobello mushrooms

Zesty, lemony pork chops and earthy portobello mushrooms cooked on the grill taste great together. Tabbouleh & Vegetable Salad (page 71) is a very good accompaniment to this dish.

**SERVES 6**

JUICE OF 1 LEMON
1 TEASPOON HERBES DE PROVENCE
2 TEASPOONS PLUS 2 TABLESPOONS EXTRA-VIRGIN OLIVE OIL
KOSHER SALT AND FRESHLY GROUND BLACK PEPPER
6 CENTER-CUT PORK CHOPS (ABOUT 3 POUNDS),
   ABOUT ¾ INCH THICK
6 LARGE PORTOBELLO MUSHROOMS, STEMMED

1. In a small bowl, whisk together the lemon juice, herbes de Provence, 2 teaspoons of olive oil, and salt and pepper to taste.

2. Put the pork chops in a nonreactive baking dish and pour the lemon mixture over them. Let the pork chops marinate in the refrigerator for about ½ hour.

3. Put the mushrooms in a large bowl and toss with the remaining 2 tablespoons of olive oil and salt and pepper to taste.

4. Prepare a gas or charcoal grill. Spray the grill rack with cooking spray. When the fire is medium–hot, and the coals are covered with a light coating of ash and glow deep red, grill the pork chops until lightly browned, about 4 minutes per side, and the mushrooms until golden and lightly charred, 4 to 5 minutes per side.

5. Cut the mushrooms into thick slices and serve over the pork chops.

• *Nutritional content per serving: 6 servings per recipe: Cals.: 293; % of cals. from fat: 49; Fat: 16g; Sat. fat: 4g; Carbs: 2g; Fiber: 0g; Sugars: 5g; Cholesterol: 94mg; Protein: 34g; Sodium: 266mg*

# Father's Day Barbecue

Herbed Goat Cheese Spread
(page 19)

Oven-Baked Pita Crisps
(page 18)

Grilled Lamb with Yogurt Sauce

(page 135)

Grilled Eggplant & Bell Peppers

(page 168)

Herbed Couscous

(page 192)

Greek Salad
with Lemon-Garlic Vinaigrette

(page 56)

Orange Angel Food Cake
with Fresh Strawberry Rhubarb Sauce

(page 201)

# pork loin
# with lemon marmalade glaze

For flavorful, savory roasts, few meats surpass pork loin. It's low in fat, cooks in less than 2 hours, and blends well with any number of basting sauces and glazes. It is particularly good with Lemon Marmalade Glaze. Served with spring vegetables and tiny new potatoes, it is a lovely alternative to ham or lamb for Easter dinner.

**SERVES 6 TO 8**

1 BONELESS CENTER-CUT PORK LOIN (3½ TO 4 POUNDS)
1 TABLESPOON OLIVE OIL
2 TEASPOONS FRESH ROSEMARY LEAVES OR 1 TEASPOON DRIED
KOSHER SALT AND FRESHLY GROUND BLACK PEPPER
1 CUP DRY WHITE WINE
1 CUP WATER
¼ CUP LEMON MARMALADE

1. Preheat the oven to 350°F.

2. Put the pork loin on a rack in a shallow roasting pan. Brush the meat with olive oil and then sprinkle it with rosemary and salt and pepper to taste. Pour the wine and water into the roasting pan. Roast in the oven for 1 hour.

3. Remove the pan from the oven and spoon ½ cup of pan drippings into a small bowl. Add the marmalade to the drippings and mix well. Pour this mixture over the meat and return it to the oven.

4. Continue roasting the meat until a meat thermometer reaches 160°F, 35 to 45 minutes, basting it 2 to 3 times with pan drippings.

5. Let the meat rest for 15 minutes before serving. Skim any fat from the pan drippings and serve with the roast.

• *Nutritional content per serving: 6 to 8 servings per recipe: Cals.: 378; % of cals. from fat: 28; Fat: 12g; Sat. fat: 4g; Carbs: 5g; Fiber: 0g; Sugars: 4g; Cholesterol: 153mg; Protein: 55g; Sodium: 308mg*

# A Winter Holiday Dinner

**Wild Mushroom Consommé**
(page 43)

**Pork Loin
with Lemon Marmalade Glaze**
(page 140)

**Creamy Braised Fennel**
(page 171)

**Warm Lentils & Sautéed Spinach**
(page 183)

**Gingerbread–Spice Cake**
(page 204)

# pan-seared pork
# with cider & dijon mustard sauce

In this dish, pork cutlets are lightly simmered in a sauce of apple cider and Dijon mustard, to create a great combination of flavors. Add Garlicky Greens (page 176) and Wild Rice & Toasted Almonds (page 191) for a super dinner.

**SERVES 6**

1½ POUNDS PORK CUTLETS (ALSO KNOWN AS
   BONELESS LOIN PORK CHOPS), ABOUT ½ INCH THICK
KOSHER SALT AND FRESHLY GROUND BLACK PEPPER
3 TEASPOONS OLIVE OIL
2 LARGE SHALLOTS, FINELY MINCED
1½ CUPS APPLE CIDER
2 TABLESPOONS DIJON MUSTARD
½ CUP CHOPPED FRESH FLAT-LEAF PARSLEY

1. Put the cutlets on a plate and pat dry. Season generously with salt and pepper.

2. In a large skillet or sauté pan, heat 1 teaspoon of the oil over medium-high heat. Add half of the pork cutlets and cook until lightly browned outside and no longer pink inside, about 2 minutes per side. Transfer to a plate and keep warm in the oven. Sauté the remaining cutlets in another teaspoon of oil; add to the previous batch.

3. Add the remaining teaspoon of oil to the skillet. Add the shallots and cook, stirring, until softened, about 2 minutes. Add the cider and mustard. Bring to a boil, stirring and scraping up any browned bits. Cook until the liquid is reduced by half, about 3 minutes. Add the parsley, stir, and cook for an additional minute. Season to taste with additional salt and pepper, if desired.

4. Arrange the pork on a serving dish and spoon the sauce over. Serve at once.

• *Nutritional content per serving: 6 servings per recipe: Cals.: 223; % of cals. from fat: 49; Fat: 12g; Sat. fat: 4g; Carbs: 9g; Fiber: 0g; Sugars: 7g; Cholesterol: 55mg; Protein: 19g; Sodium: 356mg*

# pan-seared salmon
# with lemon-soy sauce

Versatile and delicious salmon is rich in nutrients such as omega-3 fatty acids, protein, potassium, and vitamins B and D. When purchasing salmon for this recipe, it is best to buy a large piece of wild salmon and have your fishmonger cut it into 6-ounce fillets for serving. This simple-to-prepare fish dish is wonderful served over a bed of Sautéed Garlic & Orange Spinach (page 177).

**SERVES 6**

2 TABLESPOONS FRESH LEMON JUICE
3 TABLESPOONS LOW-SODIUM SOY SAUCE
3 TABLESPOONS FISH SAUCE (NAM PLA)
6 SALMON FILLETS (6 OUNCES EACH)
2 TABLESPOONS SAFFLOWER OIL

1.  In a small bowl, whisk together the lemon juice, soy sauce, and fish sauce. Put the salmon in a large shallow baking dish or bowl and pour the lemon and soy mixture over the fillets. Cover and refrigerate for 30 minutes to 1 hour.

2.  In a large nonstick skillet, heat the oil over medium-high heat. Add the salmon fillets and reduce the heat to medium. Cook the salmon until well browned and cooked through, 4 to 5 minutes per side. Serve at once.

• *Nutritional content per serving: 6 servings per recipe: Cals.: 223; % of cals. from fat: 49; Fat: 12g; Sat. fat: 4g; Carbs: 9g; Fiber: 0g; Sugars: 7g; Cholesterol: 55mg; Protein: 19g; Sodium: 356mg*

# grilled swordfish
# with spicy mango salsa

Swordfish cooked on the grill is very popular with almost everyone
and you won't go wrong serving it with Spicy Mango Salsa for a festive
summer dinner party.

**SERVES 6**

**SPICY MANGO SALSA:**
2 SMALL TOMATOES, DICED
½ RED OR YELLOW PEPPER, SEEDED, DEVEINED, AND DICED
2 SCALLIONS, TRIMMED AND MINCED (WHITE AND LIGHT GREEN PARTS)
½ RED ONION, DICED
1 RIPE MANGO, PEELED AND DICED
¼ CUP CHOPPED FRESH CILANTRO
¼ CUP CHOPPED FRESH FLAT-LEAF PARSLEY
1 TABLESPOON ORANGE JUICE
1 TABLESPOON FRESH LIME JUICE
PINCH OF RED PEPPER FLAKES
KOSHER SALT AND FRESHLY GROUND BLACK PEPPER

6 SWORDFISH STEAKS (8 OUNCES EACH), 1 INCH THICK
OLIVE OIL, FOR BRUSHING

1. To make the salsa, combine the tomatoes, pepper, scallions, onion,
mango, cilantro, parsley, orange juice, lime juice, red pepper flakes, and salt
and pepper to taste together in a bowl and mix well. Taste and adjust the
seasonings. The salsa will keep, covered, in the refrigerator for up to 3 days.

2. Prepare a gas or charcoal grill. Brush the fish lightly with the oil and
sprinkle with salt and pepper to taste. When the fire is medium-hot, and
the coals are covered with a light coating of ash and glow deep red, grill
the fish over medium-high heat until the fish is opaque throughout, 4 to 5
minutes per side.

3. Spoon the salsa over each steak and serve at once.

• *Nutritional content per serving: 6 servings per recipe: Cals.: 372; % of cals. from fat: 38; Fat: 16g;
Sat. fat:1g; Carbs: 9g; Fiber: 2g; Sugars: 7g; Cholesterol: 88mg; Protein: 46g; Sodium: 399mg*

# grilled tuna
# with tomato-cilantro salsa

Salsas aren't just for dipping with tortilla chips. They are healthy and wonderful accompaniments to grilled fish and meats too. When making this salsa, be sure to give it time to mellow before serving, but for fresh flavor and crisp texture, serve on the same day it's made.

**SERVES 6**

**TOMATO-CILANTRO SALSA:**

1 TABLESPOON DRY MUSTARD

¼ CUP WHITE WINE VINEGAR

3 TABLESPOONS EXTRA-VIRGIN OLIVE OIL

3 MEDIUM TOMATOES (ABOUT 2 POUNDS), COARSELY CHOPPED

1 RED BELL PEPPER, SEEDED, DEVEINED, AND FINELY CHOPPED

1 YELLOW BELL PEPPER, SEEDED, DEVEINED, AND FINELY CHOPPED

4 SCALLIONS, TRIMMED AND FINELY CHOPPED
 (WHITE AND LIGHT GREEN PARTS)

½ CUP FINELY CHOPPED FRESH CILANTRO

KOSHER SALT AND FRESHLY GROUND BLACK PEPPER

6 TUNA STEAKS (ABOUT 2½ POUNDS), 1 INCH THICK

1. To make the salsa, whisk the mustard and vinegar together in a small bowl. Slowly add the olive oil, whisking constantly, until the vinaigrette thickens. Stir in the tomatoes, peppers, scallions, and cilantro and mix well. Season with salt and pepper to taste. Let the salsa sit at room temperature for at least 2 hours to give the flavors time to blend.

2. Prepare a gas or charcoal grill. When the fire is medium-hot, and the coals are covered with a light coating of ash and glow deep red, grill the tuna until flaky but still moist, 6 to 7 minutes per side.

3. Spoon some salsa into the center of each plate. Place a tuna steak on top of it and spoon more salsa over the fish. Serve immediately.

• *Nutritional content per serving: 6 servings per recipe: Cals.: 366; % of cals. from fat: 50; Fat: 19g; Sat. fat: 1g; Carbs: 7g; Fiber: 2g; Sugars: 4g; Cholesterol: 73mg; Protein: 45g; Sodium: 273mg*

# shrimp stir-fry
# with asian chili sauce

This simple and delicious stir-fry is an excellent dish to serve at a dinner party, or for an easy weeknight family dinner. Seek out Asian chili sauce and fish sauce, also known as nam pla, in Asian markets, health food stores, and international sections of supermarkets. If you can't find it, use regular chili sauce and a dash of red pepper flakes.

**SERVES 6**

ONE 2-INCH PIECE OF GINGER, PEELED AND THINLY SLICED
3 GARLIC CLOVES, PEELED AND THINLY SLICED
2 SHALLOTS, PEELED AND CHOPPED
2 TABLESPOONS ASIAN CHILI SAUCE OR REGULAR CHILI SAUCE
PINCH OF DRIED RED PEPPER FLAKES (OPTIONAL)
2 TABLESPOONS FRESH LIME JUICE
2 TABLESPOONS FISH SAUCE (NAM PLA)
2 TEASPOONS LOW-SODIUM SOY SAUCE
2 TABLESPOONS WATER
2 TABLESPOONS CORN, CANOLA, OR GRAPESEED OIL
2 POUNDS MEDIUM SHRIMP (ABOUT 32 TO 36 PER POUND),
    PEELED AND DEVEINED
3 SCALLIONS, TRIMMED AND MINCED (WHITE AND LIGHT GREEN PARTS),
    FOR GARNISH

1. Put the ginger, garlic, and shallots in a food processor and process until minced. Set aside.

2. In a small bowl, whisk together the chili sauce, red pepper flakes, if using, lime juice, fish sauce, soy sauce, and water. Set aside.

3. Heat the oil in a wok or large skillet over medium-high heat until hot. Add the minced spices and cook, stirring constantly, for 1 minute. Add the sauce and stir well. Add the shrimp and coat with the sauce. Cook until the sauce is bubbling and the shrimp turns pink, about 5 minutes. Garnish with the scallions and serve at once.

• *Nutritional content per serving: 6 servings per recipe: Cals.: 183 % of cals. from fat: 32; Fat: 7g; Sat. fat: 1g; Carbs: 4g; Fiber: 1g; Sugars: 2g; Cholesterol: 179mg; Protein: 25g; Sodium: 835mg*

# Stir-Fry Supper

**Shrimp Stir-Fry with Asian Chili Sauce**
(page 148)

**Brown Rice**

**Broccoli with Asian Vinaigrette**
(page 165)

**Baby Bok Choy & Shiitake Mushrooms**
(page 166)

**Grilled Bananas & Pineapple**
(page 216)

# spicy shrimp & bell pepper creole

Shrimp Creole is traditionally made with green peppers, but this recipe uses sweeter red and yellow peppers that complement the shrimp perfectly. This is a good make-ahead dinner party dish because the tomato and vegetable broth can be cooked up to 2 days ahead of time and the shrimp can be added to it at the last minute. It is very tasty served with nutty brown rice.

**SERVES 6**

2 TABLESPOONS OLIVE OIL

1 MEDIUM ONION, FINELY CHOPPED

3 GARLIC CLOVES, THINLY SLICED

1 RED BELL PEPPER, SEEDED, DEVEINED, AND DICED

1 YELLOW BELL PEPPER, SEEDED, DEVEINED, AND DICED

1 CELERY STALK, THINLY SLICED

PINCH OF DRIED RED PEPPER FLAKES

PINCH OF CAYENNE PEPPER

4 MEDIUM RIPE TOMATOES, COARSELY CHOPPED,
   OR 1 (28-OUNCE) CAN PLUM TOMATOES WITH THEIR JUICE,
   COARSELY CHOPPED

1 CUP CLAM JUICE

1 CUP 99% FAT-FREE CHICKEN BROTH

1 TEASPOON CHOPPED FRESH THYME OR ½ TEASPOON DRIED

KOSHER SALT AND FRESHLY GROUND BLACK PEPPER

2 POUNDS LARGE SHRIMP, SHELLED AND DEVEINED

DASH OF HOT SAUCE

3 CUPS COOKED BROWN RICE, FOR SERVING

¼ CUP CHOPPED FRESH FLAT-LEAF PARSLEY, FOR GARNISH

1. In a large soup pot or Dutch oven, heat the oil over medium heat. Add the onion and garlic and cook, stirring, until golden, about 5 minutes. Add the peppers, celery, red pepper flakes, and cayenne pepper and cook, stirring occasionally, for 5 minutes.

2.  Add the tomatoes, clam juice, broth, thyme, and salt and pepper to taste. Bring to a boil, reduce the heat, cover and simmer over low heat, stirring occasionally, for 25 to 30 minutes. (The dish can be prepared up to this point and refrigerated for up to 2 days. Reheat before proceeding.)

3.  Bring the tomato and vegetable mixture to a medium boil. Add the shrimp and hot sauce, cook over medium heat until the shrimp turn pink and are cooked through, 5 to 7 minutes.

4.  Serve in large shallow bowls over rice, garnished with parsley.

• *Nutritional content per serving: 6 servings per recipe: Cals.: 319; % of cals. from fat: 22; Fat: 8g; Sat. fat: 1g; Carbs: 33g; Fiber: 4g; Sugars: 6g; Cholesterol: 180mg; Protein: 29g; Sodium: 681mg*

# roasted stuffed peppers with fresh corn & zucchini

These vegetable-stuffed red bell peppers make a lovely light meal or side dish and they also make great use of ubiquitous late-summer zucchini. Partially cooking the peppers first is necessary to ensure that they are completely cooked when served.

**SERVES 6**

6 LARGE RED BELL PEPPERS, HALVED LENGTHWISE,
   SEEDED BUT STEMS INTACT
2 TEASPOONS OLIVE OIL
1 MEDIUM RED ONION, FINELY CHOPPED
2 GARLIC CLOVES, THINLY SLICED
2 JALAPEÑO PEPPERS, SEEDED AND MINCED
1½ POUNDS SMALL ZUCCHINI, TRIMMED AND DICED
   (ABOUT 4 ZUCCHINI)
2 CUPS FRESH CORN KERNELS (2 TO 3 EARS)
½ CUP CHOPPED FRESH CILANTRO
½ CUP CHOPPED FRESH FLAT-LEAF PARSLEY
KOSHER SALT AND FRESHLY GROUND BLACK PEPPER
3 OUNCES LOW-FAT MONTEREY JACK CHEESE,
   GRATED (ABOUT ⅔ CUP)

1.  Preheat the oven to 450°F. Lightly oil a baking sheet and a 9 x 13-inch baking dish.

2.  Put the peppers, cut side down, on the baking sheet and bake for 8 to 10 minutes, until just tender. Remove the peppers from the oven and reduce the oven temperature to 375°F. Arrange the peppers, cut side up, in the baking dish.

3.  In a large skillet, heat the olive oil over medium heat. Add the onion and cook, stirring occasionally, until softened, 3 to 5 minutes. Add the garlic and jalapeños and cook, stirring, for about 1 minute. Add the zucchini and corn, cover, and cook, stirring occasionally, until the vegetables are tender, about 10 minutes. Stir in the cilantro and parsley and season with salt and pepper to taste.

**4.** Spoon about ¾ cup of filling into each pepper half. Sprinkle each with cheese. (At this point, the peppers can be allowed to cool to room temperature, covered, and refrigerated for up to 24 hours.)

**5.** Add about 2 tablespoons of water into the dish, cover with foil, and bake the peppers until heated through, about 20 minutes. Uncover and bake until the cheese is soft and melted, about 5 minutes longer. Serve at once.

• *Nutritional content per serving: 6 servings per recipe: Cals.: 177; % of cals. from fat: 22; Fat: 5g; Sat. fat: 2g; Carbs: 28g; Fiber: 7g; Sugars: 16g; Cholesterol: 10mg; Protein: 10g; Sodium: 332mg*

## THE CLEVER COOK
## ZUCCHINI

A common lament among vegetable gardeners late in the growing season is, "What can I do with all the zucchini choking the garden?" Luckily, this most popular member of the summer squash family can be eaten raw, sliced and sautéed, layered in casseroles, pureed for soups, or shredded and baked into quick breads and muffins. Zucchini is best in its season, recently harvested from a local farm or garden. Once you taste it, you'll be glad this low-carb vegetable is so versatile.

# spicy vegetarian chili with assorted condiments

Chili is a great dish to make for a hungry crowd. This recipe is loaded with beans and pan-roasted spices, as well as good-quality canned tomatoes and vegetable broth. Served buffet-style, with bowls of condiments such as chopped peppers, scallions, and herbs, avocados, and low-fat sour cream, it's always a big hit.

**SERVES 8**

1½ CUP EACH DRIED BLACK AND SMALL KIDNEY BEANS

3 TABLESPOONS OLIVE OIL

2 MEDIUM ONIONS, THINLY SLICED

6 GARLIC CLOVES, THINLY SLICED

4 SCALLIONS, TRIMMED AND MINCED
  (WHITE AND LIGHT GREEN PARTS)

3 CELERY RIBS, FINELY DICED

2 JALAPEÑO PEPPERS, SEEDED AND MINCED

1 (28-OUNCE) CAN PLUM TOMATOES WITH THEIR JUICE,
  COARSELY CHOPPED

1½ TABLESPOONS GROUND CUMIN

1½ TABLESPOONS GROUND CORIANDER

1½ TABLESPOONS PAPRIKA

1½ TABLESPOONS CHILI POWDER

PINCH OF RED PEPPER FLAKES

3 CUPS VEGETABLE BROTH

KOSHER SALT AND FRESHLY GROUND BLACK PEPPER

½ CUP CHOPPED FRESH FLAT-LEAF PARSLEY

½ CUP CHOPPED FRESH CILANTRO

FOR GARNISH: GRATED CHEDDAR CHEESE, CHOPPED RED ONIONS,
  SCALLIONS, RED, YELLOW, AND GREEN PEPPERS, AVOCADOS,
  CILANTRO, PARSLEY, AND LOW-FAT SOUR CREAM

*continued*

1. Rinse the beans and place in a large bowl. Cover with cold water and soak for up to 6 hours or overnight. Rinse and drain. Place the beans in a large pot and cover with fresh salted water. Bring to a boil over medium-high heat and simmer until just tender, about 1 hour, skimming off any foam that rises to the surface.

2. While the beans are cooking, heat the olive oil in a large soup pot and add the onions, garlic, scallions, and celery and cook over medium heat, stirring occasionally, until soft and translucent, about 10 minutes. Stir in the jalapeños and cook 5 minutes more. Add the tomatoes, bring to a boil, then simmer over low heat, stirring occasionally, about 5 minutes.

3. Place the cumin, coriander, paprika, chili powder, and red pepper flakes in a nonstick skillet and cook over medium-low heat, stirring often, until fragrant. Add the spice mixture, broth, and salt and pepper to taste to the onion and tomato mixture and stir well. Simmer over low heat until the beans are done.

4. Add the beans to the pot and stir well. Simmer over low heat for about 30 minutes. If the mixture seems too dry, add a bit of broth or water. (You can make the chili ahead up to this point. Cover and refrigerate for up to 3 days before serving.)

5. About 5 minutes before serving, stir in the parsley and cilantro. Taste and adjust the seasonings. Serve warm with desired condiments.

• *Nutritional content per serving without condiments: 8 serving per recipe: Cals.: 176; % of cals. from fat: 33; Fat: 7g; Sat. fat: 1g; Carbs: 25g; Fiber: 8g; Sugars: 8g; Cholesterol: 0mg; Protein: 8g; Sodium: 827mg*

# soba noodles
# with swiss chard & pine nuts

Sautéed Swiss chard and toasted pine nuts taste great with soba noodles.
Soba noodles are thin buckwheat noodles similar to vermicelli. They
cook very quickly so it is best to have everything ready when preparing
this dish.

**SERVES 6**

1 TABLESPOON OLIVE OIL
2 GARLIC CLOVES, THINLY SLICED
1½ POUNDS SWISS CHARD, STEMMED, RINSED, DRAINED,
　　AND CUT INTO ½-INCH STRIPS
2 TABLESPOONS LOW-SODIUM SOY SAUCE
1 POUND SOBA NOODLES
PINCH OF RED PEPPER FLAKES
FRESHLY GROUND BLACK PEPPER
3 TABLESPOONS PINE NUTS, TOASTED (SEE NOTE)

1.  Heat the oil in a large sauté pan over medium heat. Add the garlic and
cook, stirring, until golden brown, about 3 minutes. Add the chard and the
soy sauce and stir well. Cover the pan and continue to cook until the chard
is wilted and tender, about 15 minutes.

2.  Meanwhile, bring a large pot of water to a boil. Add the noodles and
cook until tender, about 3 minutes. Drain, reserving ¾ cup of the cooking
liquid. Stir the liquid into the chard and add the pepper flakes and pepper.

3.  Divide the noodles among 6 bowls and spoon the chard mixture over
them. Sprinkle each serving with the toasted pine nuts and serve at once.

**Note:** To toast the pine nuts, spread them on a baking sheet and toast
them in a preheated 350°F oven or toaster oven until golden and fragrant,
3 to 5 minutes. Shake the pan once or twice for even toasting. Slide the
nuts off the baking sheet as soon as they reach the desired color to stop the
cooking. Let them cool.

  • *Nutritional content per serving: 6 servings per recipe: Cals.: 323; % of cals. from fat: 17; Fat: 6g;
Sat. fat: 1g; Carbs: 54g; Fiber: 6g; Sugars: 4g; Cholesterol: 0mg; Protein: 14g; Sodium: 944mg*

## GRITS, GROATS, & BUCKWHEAT

Buckwheat is loaded with
protein and other
nutrients, and is often
ground into a dark flour
to make everything from
pancakes to soba noodles.
In eastern Europe
buckwheat is crushed into
small groats, which are
eaten as a side dish or a
breakfast cereal.
Buckwheat grits are finely
ground groats that are
used to make a cream of
buckwheat cereal. Kasha
is the Russian name for
toasted buckwheat groats.

# mediterranean-style baked pasta

This is a good hearty pasta dish made with sautéed eggplant, zucchini, and red peppers. All you need is a salad of fresh mixed greens to round out the meal.

**SERVES 6 TO 8**

½ CUP PLAIN BREADCRUMBS
1 TABLESPOON OLIVE OIL
2 SMALL ZUCCHINI, TRIMMED, PEELED, AND CUT INTO ½-INCH DICE
1 MEDIUM EGGPLANT, TRIMMED, PEELED, AND CUT INTO ½-INCH DICE
1 RED BELL PEPPER, SEEDED, DEVEINED, AND FINELY CHOPPED
1 STALK CELERY, FINELY CHOPPED
1 GARLIC CLOVE, MINCED
¼ CUP DRY WHITE WINE
1 (28-OUNCE) CAN PLUM TOMATOES WITH THEIR JUICE,
   COARSELY CHOPPED
KOSHER SALT AND FRESHLY GROUND BLACK PEPPER
1 POUND DRIED PASTA, SUCH AS PENNE, PENNE RIGATE,
   OR RIGATONI
1½ CUPS GRATED PART-SKIM MOZZARELLA CHEESE
2 LARGE EGGS, LIGHTLY BEATEN
2 TABLESPOONS FRESHLY GRATED PARMESAN CHEESE

**1.** Preheat the oven to 375°F. Lightly oil a 3-quart baking dish. Coat the dish with ¼ cup of the breadcrumbs, tapping out the excess.

**2.** In a large nonstick skillet, heat the oil over medium-high heat. Add the zucchini, eggplant, bell pepper, and celery and cook, stirring, until tender, about 10 minutes. Add the garlic and cook, stirring, for 1 minute. Add the wine and cook, stirring, until almost evaporated, about 2 minutes. Add the tomatoes and their juice. Bring to a simmer and cook, stirring occasionally, until thickened, 10 to 12 minutes. Season to taste with salt and pepper. Transfer to a large bowl and let cool to room temperature.

**3.** Meanwhile, bring a large pot of salted water to a boil. Add the pasta and cook until al dente, 8 to 10 minutes, or according to package directions. Drain and let cool. Toss the pasta with the vegetable mixture. Stir in the mozzarella cheese and toss again.

**4.** Spoon the pasta mixture into the prepared baking dish and drizzle the eggs evenly over the top. In a small bowl, combine the remaining ¼ cup breadcrumbs and the Parmesan cheese. Sprinkle evenly over the pasta.

**5.** Bake the pasta until golden and bubbly, about 40 to 50 minutes. Let stand for 10 minutes before serving.

• *Nutritional content per serving: 8 servings per recipe: Cals.:372; % of cals. from fat: 20; Fat: 8g; Sat. fat: 3g; Carbs: 59g; Fiber: 5g; Sugars: 8g; Cholesterol: 66mg; Protein: 17g; Sodium: 448mg*

# onions

Onions are an essential component of many dishes because of the zip or sweetness they provide. Raw, sautéed, fried, baked, stuffed, skewered, or creamed, there seems to be almost nothing a willing onion won't do—and do well. Today there are more varieties of onions than ever before. In addition to traditional yellow onions that are great for cooking, but too pungent for most people to eat raw, there are the slightly sweeter white and red onions. And geat flavor is not all that members of the onion family bring to the table: they contain powerful antioxidants that are helpful in keeping the cardiovascular system healthy.

## SWEET
These include Vidalia, Maui, Texas Spring Sweet, and Walla Walla. These are perfect for sandwiches and salads and offer a milder touch in cooked dishes.

## GREEN
Leeks add their own gentler flavor to stir-fries, stews, soups, and casseroles. Scallions are also great in stir-fries—cooked very quickly over high heat for only a minute or so—and in salads. And ramps are the springtime favorites that look like baby leeks but pack a wild intense flavor.

## PEARL
Pearl onions usually only make an appearance on tables around the winter holidays, but they are a tasty touch to add to casseroles year-round. If you boil them, cut an "X" through the bottom so you can pop off the skin easily once they are cooked.

## ALL IN THE FAMILY
Shallots and garlic. Shallots are wonderful minced into a salad dressing or a piquant dipping sauce. Roasted or creamed they add a special flavor to a standard dish. As for garlic—which makes its appearance in many cuisines and can spark up almost any dish, whether meat, vegetable, or grain—it is worth looking for local and farm-grown varieties. In most grocery stores there is only one kind—but there are many varieties and each has its own unique flavor. If you have the chance, experiment with the artichoke, rocambole, porcelain, and purple stripe varieties of garlic.

chapter six **side dishes**

S ometimes the best meals are made up of terrific side dishes alone—at a restaurant it's often fun to order and split a few appetizers and sides and skip the main course altogether. When entertaining at home these same kinds of dishes offer you a way to dress up the main course. Serve roast chicken with Creamy Braised Fennel and Roasted Root Vegetables or grilled fish with Baby Bok Choy & Shiitake Mushrooms or Sautéed Chickpeas & Swiss Chard. Simple entrées are also terrific when a variety of sides are offered in a buffet—easy for you, sumptuous for your guests.

# broccoli with asian vinaigrette

In this recipe, broccoli florets and stems are lightly steamed and tossed together with vinaigrette made with sesame oil, rice vinegar, and soy sauce. This side dish is delicious served warm, cold, or at room temperature.

**SERVES 6**

1 LARGE BUNCH BROCCOLI
¼ CUP TOASTED SESAME OIL
¼ CUP RICE VINEGAR
1 TABLESPOON LOW-SODIUM SOY SAUCE
½ TEASPOON SUGAR
PINCH OF RED PEPPER FLAKES

1.  Separate the broccoli into small florets. Cut off and peel the stalks and cut them on the diagonal into ½-inch pieces.

2.  Steam the broccoli over simmering water until crisp-tender, 6 to 8 minutes. Remove from the heat and drain. Transfer the broccoli to a shallow serving bowl.

3.  In a small bowl, whisk together the oil, vinegar, soy sauce, sugar, and red pepper flakes until well combined. Taste and adjust the seasonings, if necessary. Pour the vinaigrette over the broccoli and toss lightly to coat.

4.  Serve the broccoli warm or at room temperature. The broccoli can also be chilled for a few hours before serving.

• *Nutritional content per serving: 6 servings per recipe: Cals.: 99; % of cals. from fat: 84; Fat: 9g; Sat. fat: 1g; Carbs: 4g; Fiber: 2g; Sugars: 2g; Cholesterol: 0mg; Protein: 2g; Sodium: 81mg*

# baby bok choy & shiitake mushrooms

Bok choy is a mild-tasting and versatile vegetable, and it pairs very nicely with shiitake mushrooms. Baby bok choy is more tender, but if you cannot find it, it's fine to use regular bok choy in this dish. Be sure to have all of your ingredients ready for this quick stir-fry.

**SERVES 6**

**STIR-FRY SAUCE:**

½ CUP 99% FAT-FREE CHICKEN BROTH
2 TABLESPOONS ASIAN FISH SAUCE (NAM PLA)
1 TEASPOON LOW-SODIUM SOY SAUCE

2 TABLESPOONS CANOLA OIL
2 GARLIC CLOVES, THINLY SLICED
2 TABLESPOONS MINCED FRESH GINGER
1 CUP SHIITAKE MUSHROOMS, STEMMED AND THINLY SLICED
2 POUNDS BABY BOK CHOY, LEAVES AND STEMS
   RINSED, DRAINED, AND CUT INTO 1-INCH PIECES

1. To make the stir-fry sauce, whisk together the broth, fish sauce, and soy sauce in a samll bowl and set aside.

2. In a large skillet or wok, heat the oil over high heat until very hot. Add the garlic and ginger and cook, stirring, for about 30 seconds. Add the mushrooms and cook, stirring, for about 2 minutes. Add the bok choy and cook, stirring, until crisp-tender, about 3 minutes.

3. Add the Stir-Fry Sauce and cook, stirring occasionally, until the bok choy is tender but still bright green and the sauce is slightly reduced, about 3 minutes longer. Serve immediately.

• *Nutritional content per serving: 6 servings per recipe: Cals.: 81; % of cals. from fat: 54; Fat: 5g; Sat. fat: trace; Carbs 7g; Fiber 2g; Sugars: 4g; Cholesterol: 0mg; Protein: 3g; Sodium: 768mg*

# roasted cauliflower

Cauliflower may be an acquired taste for some people, but when it is roasted and tossed with a zesty blend of warm olive oil and capers, it takes on a delicious nutty flavor that is hard for anyone to pass up. Serve this on the side with almost any dish or as part of an antipasto platter.

**SERVES 6**

2 HEADS CAULIFLOWER, CUT INTO FLORETS
KOSHER SALT AND FRESHLY GROUND BLACK PEPPER
5 TABLESPOONS EXTRA-VIRGIN OLIVE OIL
1 TABLESPOON FRESHLY GRATED LEMON ZEST
2 GARLIC CLOVES, THINLY SLICED
2 TABLESPOONS DRAINED CAPERS
LEMON WEDGES, FOR GARNISH

1. Preheat the oven to 350°F.
2. Put the cauliflower in a large bowl and season to taste with salt and pepper. Pour 2 tablespoons of the olive oil over it and toss well. Spread the cauliflower on a baking sheet and roast, turning occasionally, until tender and golden brown, about 45 minutes. Transfer to a large bowl.
3. Meanwhile, combine 3 tablespoons of the olive oil, the lemon zest, and garlic in a small saucepan and cook over low heat, stirring occasionally, for about 20 minutes.
4. Pour the warm olive oil over the cauliflower mixture and toss. Add the capers and toss again. Season to taste with additional black pepper. Serve on a platter, garnished with lemon wedges.

• *Nutritional content per serving: 6 servings per recipe: Cals.: 116; % of cals. from fat: 88; Fat: 11g; Sat. fat: 2g; Carbs: 4g; Fiber: 2g; Sugars: 2g; Cholesterol: 0mg; Protein: 1g; Sodium: 295mg*

# grilled eggplant & bell peppers

These very tasty grilled eggplant and red bell peppers are delicious served with grilled lamb—they're also very good tucked into a warm pita with yogurt dressing (see Grilled Lamb & Cucumber Raita Pitas, page 96).

**SERVES 6**

¼ CUP OLIVE OIL
1 GARLIC CLOVE, THINLY SLICED
KOSHER SALT AND FRESHLY GROUND BLACK PEPPER
1 LARGE EGGPLANT, UNPEELED, TRIMMED,
   AND SLICED INTO ¼-INCH-THICK ROUNDS
1 LARGE RED BELL PEPPER, STEMMED, SEEDED,
   AND QUARTERED
1 LARGE YELLOW BELL PEPPER, STEMMED, SEEDED,
   AND QUARTERED

1. Whisk the olive oil, garlic, and salt and pepper to taste together in a small bowl. Brush the eggplant and peppers with the mixture.

2. Prepare a gas or charcoal grill. When the fire is medium-hot, and the coals are covered with a light coating of ash and glow deep red, put the eggplant on the grill and cook until golden brown, 3 to 4 minutes per side. After about 2 minutes, add the peppers and cook until lightly charred, 2 to 3 minutes per side.

3. Drizzle the eggplant and peppers with a bit of extra-virgin olive oil and additional salt and pepper, if desired, and serve warm or at room temperature.

• *Nutritional content per serving: 6 servings per recipe: Cals.: 135; % of cals. from fat: 63; Fat: 9g; Sat. fat: 1g; Carbs: 14g; Fiber: 4g; Sugars: 6g; Cholesterol: 0mg; Protein: 2g; Sodium: 196mg*

# sautéed carrots with black olives

Few recipes are easier to make than this one—it takes only minutes to cook. The pleasant saltiness of the olives blends nicely with the natural sweetness of the carrots, making this a piquant accompaniment to most any dish.

**SERVES 6**

1 TABLESPOON OLIVE OIL

1 POUND CARROTS, SLICED INTO ½-INCH-THICK ROUNDS

2 TABLESPOONS 99% FAT-FREE CHICKEN OR VEGETABLE BROTH

2 TABLESPOONS PITTED AND CHOPPED SALTY BLACK OLIVES,
    SUCH AS NIÇOISE, KALAMATA, OR GAETA

1. In a large sauté pan, heat the oil over medium-high heat. Add the carrots and cook, tossing to coat with the oil, until the carrots are just tender, 5 to 7 minutes.

2. Stir in the broth, cover, and cook until the carrots are tender, about 5 minutes more. Stir in the olives and serve immediately.

• *Nutritional content per serving: 6 servings per recipe: Cals.: 51; % of cals. from fat: 48; Fat: 3g; Sat. fat: trace; Carbs: 7g; Fiber: 2g; Sugars: 3g; Cholesterol: 0mg; Protein: 1g; Sodium: 91mg*

# creamy braised fennel

Here is a fabulous side dish to serve with just about any main dish.

**SERVES 6**

1 TABLESPOON OLIVE OIL
3 LEEKS (WHITE AND PALE PARTS ONLY) TRIMMED,
   WELL-RINSED, AND CUT INTO 1-INCH PIECES
½ CUP FINELY CHOPPED SHALLOTS
½ CUP DRY WHITE WINE
4 FENNEL BULBS, EACH BULB TRIMMED
   AND CUT INTO 8 WEDGES
2 CUPS LOW-FAT CHICKEN OR VEGETABLE BROTH
KOSHER SALT AND FRESHLY GROUND BLACK PEPPER
2 TEASPOONS DIJON MUSTARD
2 TABLESPOONS LOW-FAT SOUR CREAM

1. In a Dutch oven or deep sauté pan, heat the oil over medium-low heat. Add the leeks and shallots and cook, stirring, until softened but not browned, about 4 minutes. Add the wine, increase the heat to medium, and simmer for 2 minutes. Add the fennel and broth and season with salt and pepper to taste. Reduce the heat to low, cover, and simmer until the fennel is tender, about 20 minutes. Transfer the vegetables to a bowl with a slotted spoon.

2. Whisk the mustard into the cooking liquid and cook for 2 minutes. Return the reserved vegetables to the cooking liquid and cook until heated though, about 2 minutes. Remove from the heat and gently stir in the sour cream. Taste and adjust the seasonings, if necessary, and serve at once.

• *Nutritional content per serving: 6 servings per recipe: Cals.: 112; % of cals. from fat: 26; Fat: 3g; Sat. fat: 1g; Carbs: 17g; Fiber: 6g; Sugars: 5g; Cholesterol: 2mg; Protein: 3g; Sodium: 653mg*

# An Autumn
# Dinner Party

## Asparagus & Celery Salad
## with Walnut Dressing
(page 60)


## Pan-Seared Pork
## with Cider & Dijon Mustard Sauce
(page 143)

Sautéed Carrots with Black Olives
(page 170)

Wild Rice & Toasted Almonds
(page 191)

Garlicky Greens
(page 176)

Lemon–Poppy Seed Cake
(page 199)

# red cabbage & apple sauté

Cruciferous vegetables, such as cabbage, broccoli, cauliflower, and Brussels sprouts, are an excellent source of vitamin C and are very low in fat and carbohydrates. Red Cabbage & Apple Sauté is packed with nutrients and is a delicious side dish to serve with roast chicken, pork, or lamb.

**SERVES 8**

1 TABLESPOON VEGETABLE OIL

1 LARGE RED ONION, COARSELY CHOPPED

1 HEAD RED CABBAGE (2½ TO 3 POUNDS), SHREDDED

KOSHER SALT

1 GRANNY SMITH APPLE, CORED AND CHOPPED

⅓ CUP APPLE CIDER

1 TABLESPOON APPLE CIDER VINEGAR

1 TEASPOON CARAWAY SEEDS

½ CUP CHOPPED FRESH FLAT-LEAF PARSLEY, FOR GARNISH

1. In a large, nonreactive soup pot, heat the oil over medium heat, add the onion, and cook, stirring, until softened, about 3 minutes. Add the cabbage and salt to taste and toss well. Cover and steam for 10 minutes. Add the apple and toss again.

2. Meanwhile, in a small bowl, mix the cider, vinegar, and caraway seeds together. Pour over the cabbage mixture and toss well. Cover and simmer, stirring occasionally, until the cabbage is softened, about 25 to 30 minutes. Taste and adjust the seasonings, if necessary. Garnish with parsley and serve warm.

• *Nutritional content per serving: 8 servings per recipe: Cals.: 66; % of cals. from fat: 29; Fat: 2g; Sat. fat: 1g; Carbs: 12g; Fiber: 3g; Sugars: 8g; Cholesterol: 0mg; Protein:2g; Sodium: 160mg*

**POWER VEGETABLES**

Steamed vegetables retain nutrients and taste fresh and crisp. To imbue with flavor add seasoning such as fresh grated ginger, garlic, dried thyme or rosemary, soy sauce, or ancho chile powder to the steaming liquid; or steam with homemade chicken broth.

# garlicky greens

Sautéed greens and garlic go well with almost any main dish and they're also a good accompaniment to rice and grains. Try other dark leafy greens, such as watercress, Swiss chard, or mustard greens in this recipe too.

**SERVES 8**

TWO 1-POUND BUNCHES SPINACH, CLEANED AND STEMMED
TWO 1-POUND BUNCHES COLLARD GREENS,
   CLEANED AND STEMMED
ONE 1-POUND BUNCH GREEN OR PURPLE KALE,
   CLEANED AND STEMMED
1 SLICE (ABOUT 1 OUNCE) BACON, CHOPPED
1 MEDIUM ONION, CHOPPED
4 GARLIC CLOVES, THINLY SLICED
½ CUP 99% FAT-FREE CHICKEN BROTH
1 TEASPOON APPLE CIDER VINEGAR
KOSHER SALT AND FRESHLY GROUND BLACK PEPPER

1. Bring a large pot of salted water to a boil. Add the greens, reduce the heat, cover and cook over medium heat until almost tender, about 7 minutes. Drain well and let cool. Coarsely chop and set aside.

2. Cook the bacon in a large nonstick skillet over medium heat until crisp, about 5 minutes. Remove with a slotted spoon and drain on paper towels. Add the onion and garlic to the drippings in the skillet and cook, stirring frequently, until softened, about 5 minutes. Stir in the greens and toss well. Add the broth, cover and cook until the greens are tender, about 5 minutes.

3. Add the vinegar, toss to combine, and season with salt and pepper to taste. Transfer to a platter, top the greens with the bacon pieces, and serve at once.

*• Nutritional content per serving: 8 servings per recipe: Cals.: 64; % of cals. from fat: 14; Fat: 1g; Sat. fat: trace; Carbs: 12g; Fiber: 6g; Sugars: 2g; Cholesterol: 1mg; Protein: 5g; Sodium: 312mg*

# sautéed garlic & orange spinach

It turns out that your mom was right when she told you to "eat your greens." Spinach and other greens such as kale, collard greens, Swiss chard, and bok choy are packed with folate, iron, and calcium—nutrients that lower the risk of heart disease and many types of cancer. Quickly sautéed spinach with garlic and a splash of orange juice is an excellent accompaniment to salmon and other fish dishes.

**SERVES 6**

2 TABLESPOONS OLIVE OIL
2 GARLIC CLOVES, THINLY SLICED
3 TABLESPOONS ORANGE JUICE
2 (10-OUNCE) BAGS FRESH SPINACH, RINSED AND DRIED,
    STEMMED AND COARSELY CHOPPED
KOSHER SALT AND FRESHLY GROUND BLACK PEPPER

In a large sauté pan, heat the oil over medium-high heat. Add the garlic and cook, stirring constantly, until it begins to brown, about 30 seconds. Add the orange juice and cook until it reduces a bit, about 30 seconds. Add the spinach and cook, stirring constantly, until it begins to wilt. Season to taste with salt and pepper and stir well again. Serve at once.

• *Nutritional content per serving: 6 servings per recipe: Cals.: 61; % of cals. from fat: 69; Fat: 5g; Sat. fat: 1g; Carbs: 3g; Fiber: 2g; Sugars: 1g; Cholesterol: 0mg; Protein: 2g; Sodium: 248mg*

# braised pearl onions, shallots, & leeks

There is such a wide variety of onions available to the home cook today and they're wonderful to experiment with. This braised dish of pearl onions, shallots, and leeks is a very good side dish that works well in a holiday menu—it's much lighter and cleaner-tasting than traditional creamed onions.

**SERVES 6**

2 TABLESPOONS OLIVE OIL
3 GARLIC CLOVES, THINLY SLICED
16 PEARL ONIONS, PREFERABLY A MIX OF WHITE AND RED, PEELED
8 SHALLOTS, PEELED AND LEFT WHOLE
4 BABY LEEKS OR 2 LARGE LEEKS, TRIMMED, RINSED, SPLIT,
   AND CUT INTO 1-INCH PIECES
KOSHER SALT AND FRESHLY GROUND BLACK PEPPER
1½ CUPS VEGETABLE BROTH

1.  Heat the olive oil over medium heat in a large skillet fitted with a lid. Add the garlic and cook, stirring, until softened, about 3 minutes. Add the onions, shallots, and leeks, toss to coat well with the oil, add salt and pepper to taste, and cook, stirring, until just golden, about 5 minutes.

2.  Add 1 cup of the broth, bring to a boil, reduce the heat, cover, and simmer, stirring occasionally, for 10 minutes. Add the additional ½ cup of broth and cook, covered, until the onions are tender, an additional 10 minutes. Turn the heat up and cook until the liquid is reduced and thickened, 3 to 5 minutes more. Serve warm.

• *Nutritional content per serving: 6 servings per recipe: Cals.: 91; % of cals. from fat: 46; Fat: 5g; Sat. fat: 1g; Carbs: 12g; Fiber: 2g; Sugars: 5g; Cholesterol: 0mg; Protein: 1g; Sodium: 449mg*

# roasted sweet potatoes with lime & cilantro

**SWEET POTATOES VERSUS YAMS**

There is a difference and it is, nutritionally speaking, quite significant. Sweet potatoes are loaded with beta-carotene, and yams have almost none. Three-and-a-half ounces of sweet potato contains more than 8,800 IU of vitamin A or about twice the recommended daily allowance, 42% of the Recommended Daily Allowance (RDA) for vitamin C, 6% of the RDA for calcium, 10% of the RDA for iron, and 8% of the RDA for thiamine for healthy adults. It is low in sodium and is a good source of fiber. When storing sweet potatoes, put them in a dry bin where the temperature is not below 55°F. If they are refrigerated, these tropical tubers taste off when cooked.

Humble sweet potatoes may be commonplace, but they deliver plenty of satisfying flavor in all kinds of dishes. Their sweeter and more complex flavor is often an improvement over the best varieties of white potato. In this simple recipe they are roasted with a bit of olive oil, drizzled with a dash fresh lime juice, and tossed with cilantro. That's it!

**SERVES 8**

6 MEDIUM SWEET POTATOES, PEELED AND CUT INTO 2-INCH CUBES
2 TABLESPOONS EXTRA-VIRGIN OLIVE OIL
KOSHER SALT AND FRESHLY GROUND BLACK PEPPER
2 TABLESPOONS FRESH LIME JUICE
½ CUP CHOPPED FRESH CILANTRO

1. Preheat the oven to 350°F.
2. Put the sweet potatoes in a medium bowl, toss to coat with 1 tablespoon of the olive oil, and season with salt and pepper to taste.
3. Transfer the potatoes to a baking sheet and roast until they are lightly browned and can be easily pierced with a fork, about 1 hour. Remove and let cool a bit.
4. Transfer the potatoes to a large bowl. Add the remaining tablespoon of olive oil, the lime juice, and the cilantro and toss gently to combine. Taste and adjust the seasonings, if necessary. Serve warm or at room temperature.

*• Nutritional content per serving: 8 servings per recipe: Cals.: 133; % of cals. from fat: 25; Fat: 4g; Sat. fat: trace; Carbs: 24g; Fiber: 3g; Sugars: 6g; Cholesterol: 0mg; Protein: 2g; Sodium: 159mg*

# A Weeknight
# Family Dinner

Balsamic-Glazed
Roasted Chicken Breasts
(page 113)

Roasted Sweet Potatoes
with Lime & Cilantro
(page 180)

Sautéed Garlic & Orange Spinach
(page 177)

Chilled Minted Fruit
(page 228)

# roasted root vegetables

Slow-cooked root vegetables are an ideal dish for a simple autumnal meal. Gentle oven roasting allows them to caramelize and develop a full, rounded flavor. In this recipe, potatoes, carrots, parsnips, and shallots are tossed with olive oil and chicken broth and roasted for up to 2 hours. Great for advance dinner party planning—great-tasting too.

**SERVES 6**

2 POUNDS UNPEELED SMALL RED NEW POTATOES (8 TO 10),
    HALVED OR QUARTERED
12 SHALLOTS, PEELED
6 CARROTS, PEELED AND CUT INTO 1-INCH PIECES
4 PARSNIPS (ABOUT 1 POUND), PEELED
    AND CUT INTO 1-INCH ROUNDS
2 TABLESPOONS EXTRA-VIRGIN OLIVE OIL
½ CUP 99% FAT-FREE CHICKEN BROTH
1 TEASPOON CHOPPED FRESH ROSEMARY LEAVES
KOSHER SALT AND FRESHLY GROUND BLACK PEPPER

1. Preheat the oven to 300°F.

2. In a roasting pan, toss the potatoes, shallots, carrots, and parsnips with the olive oil, broth, rosemary, and salt and pepper to taste.

3. Roast until the vegetables are fork-tender, 1½ to 2 hours, tossing them 2 or 3 times during roasting.

4. Arrange the vegetables in a shallow bowl or a large platter and serve warm.

• *Nutritional content per serving: 6 servings per recipe: Cals.: 252; % of cals. from fat: 49; Fat: 5g; Sat. fat: trace; Carbs: 49g; Fiber: 8g; Sugars: 8g; Cholesterol: 0mg; Protein: 6g; Sodium: 256mg*

# warm lentils & sautéed spinach

Lentils are easy to prepare and taste great in combination with spinach or any other dark leafy green. This hearty and satisfying side dish is very good with grilled fish or chicken.

**SERVES 6**

3 TABLESPOONS OLIVE OIL
1½ CUPS DRIED LENTILS
2¼ CUPS 99% FAT-FREE CHICKEN BROTH
½ CUP WATER
2 GARLIC CLOVES, THINLY SLICED
1 (10-OUNCE) PACKAGE FRESH SPINACH, RINSED, STEMMED,
   AND COARSELY CHOPPED (ABOUT 6 CUPS)
KOSHER SALT AND FRESHLY GROUND BLACK PEPPER

1.  Heat 2 tablespoons of the olive oil in a large sauté pan over medium-high heat. Add the lentils and toss to coat with the oil.

2.  Add 2 cups of the chicken broth and the water and bring to a boil. Reduce the heat, cover, and simmer, stirring occasionally, until the lentils are just tender, 25 to 30 minutes.

3.  Heat the remaining tablespoon of olive oil in another sauté pan over medium heat. Add the garlic and cook, stirring, until tender, about 1 minute. Add the spinach and cook, stirring and tossing occasionally, until it begins to wilt, about 1 minute. Add the remaining ¼ cup of chicken broth and cook until the spinach is tender and wilted.

4.  Add the spinach and any cooking liquid to the lentils and toss together. Season with salt and pepper to taste and serve at once.

• *Nutritional content per serving: 6 servings per recipe: Cals.: 210; % of cals. from fat: 32; Fat: 8g; Sat. fat: 8g; Carbs: 25g; Fiber: 10g; Sugars: 3g; Cholesterol: 1mg; Protein: 12g; Sodium: 593mg*

# sautéed chickpeas & swiss chard

Hearty greens and beans make a wonderful side dish that goes with all types of roasts and grilled dishes. They also pack a powerful nutritional punch. This quick-cooking recipe uses canned chickpeas for convenience, but if you prefer cooked dried beans, by all means, use them.

**SERVES 6**

2 TABLESPOONS OLIVE OIL
1 MEDIUM RED ONION, THINLY SLICED
6 SCALLIONS, TRIMMED AND CUT INTO 1-INCH PIECES
   (WHITE AND LIGHT GREEN PARTS)
2 GARLIC CLOVES, THINLY SLICED
1½ POUNDS SWISS CHARD, RINSED, STEMMED,
   AND COARSELY CHOPPED
½ CUP 99% FAT-FREE CHICKEN BROTH
KOSHER SALT AND FRESHLY GROUND BLACK PEPPER
1 (15-OUNCE) CAN CHICKPEAS, RINSED AND DRAINED
PINCH OF DRIED CHILE FLAKES
2 TABLESPOONS FRESH LEMON JUICE
½ CUP CHOPPED FRESH FLAT-LEAF PARSLEY

1.  In a large skillet, heat the oil over medium heat. Add the onion, scallions, and garlic and cook, stirring often, until softened, about 5 minutes.

2.  Add the Swiss chard and toss well until coated. Add ¼ cup of the broth and salt and pepper to taste and cook, tossing well, until the chard is just wilted, about 5 minutes.

3.  Add the chickpeas and the remaining ¼ cup of broth and cook, stirring occasionally, for 2 minutes. Add the chile flakes, lemon juice, and parsley and cook, stirring often, an additional 5 minutes. Serve at once.

• *Nutritional content per serving: 6 servings per recipe: Cals.: 141; % of cals. from fat: 37; Fat: 6g; Sat. fat: 1g; Carbs: 18g; Fiber: 6g; Sugars: 4g; Cholesterol: 0mg; Protein: 6g; Sodium: 514mg*

# tomato-maple baked beans

Hints of chili sauce and maple syrup add sweetness to these delicious homemade baked beans. This is a terrific dish for a summer barbecue or picnic.

**SERVES 8**

2½ CUPS DRIED WHITE BEANS (ONE 16-OUNCE PACKAGE)
3 SLICES TURKEY BACON, COARSELY CHOPPED
2 TEASPOONS OLIVE OIL
1 LARGE ONION, COARSELY CHOPPED
4 GARLIC CLOVES, FINELY CHOPPED
1 (28-OUNCE) CAN DICED PLUM TOMATOES IN PUREE
¼ CUP CHILI SAUCE
¼ CUP APPLE CIDER VINEGAR
2 TABLESPOONS DIJON MUSTARD
2 TABLESPOONS MAPLE SYRUP
DASH OF HOT SAUCE
1 TABLESPOON FRESH THYME, FINELY CHOPPED,
    OR 1½ TEASPOONS DRIED
KOSHER SALT AND FRESHLY GROUND BLACK PEPPER
ABOUT 2 CUPS 99% FAT-FREE CHICKEN BROTH

1. Rinse the beans and put in a large bowl. Cover by about 2 inches with cold water and soak for 6 to 8 hours or overnight. Drain and set aside.

2. Preheat the oven to 350°F.

3. In a large soup pot or Dutch oven, cook the bacon over medium-high heat until lightly browned. Add the olive oil and cook the onion and garlic, stirring occasionally, until translucent, about 3 minutes.

4. Add the tomatoes, chili sauce, vinegar, mustard, maple syrup, hot sauce, thyme, and salt and pepper to taste and bring to a boil. Reduce the heat, stir well, and simmer for 5 minutes. Add the beans and 1 cup of the broth and stir well again.

**5.** Cover and bake for 1½ hours. Uncover and bake the beans an additional ½ hour as the sauce becomes reduced and thickened, adding and stirring in more broth if the beans seem too dry. (The beans can be prepared 1 day ahead and refrigerated. Reheat before serving.)

• *Nutritional content per serving: 8 servings per recipe: Cals.: 286; % of cals. from fat: 9; Fat: 3g; Sat. fat: 1g; Carbs: 50g; Fiber: 11g; Sugars: 13g; Cholesterol: 4mg; Protein: 17g; Sodium: 579mg*

## BEAN BONANZA

As good for you as they are delicious, eating a cup of cooked beans a day can lower your total cholesterol by up to 10% in 6 weeks. Though that may not seem like much, it actually decreases your risk of heart disease by 20%. One study found that only 3 weeks of increased bean intake ¾ cup of navy and pinto beans) lowered the men's cholesterol by an average of 19%. This reduces the risk of heart attack by almost 40%. Also, because of the high fiber in beans, they can curb your appetite for fattier, less healthy foods. It is also thought that the soluble fiber in beans helps to create more insulin receptor sites. These sites are like tiny docks for the insulin molecules to connect to, allowing the insulin to get to the cells that need it. Beans also provide folate and potassium, and are very high in protein and fiber but low in fat. Dried or canned beans will give you the same benefit, but canned beans are high in sodium, so be sure to drain and rinse well. Dried beans are high-carb foods and may require you to adjust your gluscose management techniques. So enjoy—in moderation.

# Fourth of July Barbecue

Guacamole
(page 13)


Handmade Spicy Tortilla Chips
(page 12)

Grilled Jerk Chicken
(page 118)

Red Cabbage, Pepper, & Onion
Slaw with Orange-Cumin Vinaigrette
(page 63)

Asparagus & Tomato Salad
with Mustard-Dill Vinaigrette
(page 58)

Tomato-Maple Baked Beans
(page 186)

Strawberry-Rhubarb Tart
(page 205)

# white bean puree

Pureed white beans are delicious with roast lamb or pork. And if you have any leftovers, this puree is excellent spread over toasted peasant bread or crackers.

**SERVES 8**

2 CUPS (1 POUND) DRIED WHITE CANNELLINI BEANS

8 CUPS WATER

2 CUPS 99% FAT-FREE CHICKEN BROTH

2 ONIONS

2 CARROTS, PEELED AND COARSELY CHOPPED

6 SPRIGS FRESH FLAT-LEAF PARSLEY

2 TABLESPOONS OLIVE OIL

6 GARLIC CLOVES, HALVED

2 TABLESPOONS CHOPPED FRESH BASIL

½ TEASPOON DRIED OREGANO

¼ TEASPOON DRIED THYME

1 TABLESPOON LOW-FAT SOUR CREAM

2 TABLESPOONS FRESH LEMON JUICE

KOSHER SALT AND FRESHLY GROUND BLACK PEPPER

1.  Pick over the beans and rinse thoroughly. Put the beans in a large bowl, add enough cold water to cover by about 2 inches and set aside to soak for 6 to 8 hours or overnight.

2.  Drain the beans and transfer them to a large soup pot. Add the water, broth, 1 of the onions, the carrots, and parsley and bring to a boil over high heat. Reduce the heat and simmer the beans, skimming any foam that rises to the surface, until just tender, 40 to 50 minutes. Be careful not to overcook. Strain the beans in a colander, discard the onion and parsley, and set the beans aside.

3. Chop the remaining onion. Heat the olive oil in a large skillet over medium heat. Add the onion and the garlic to the skillet and cook, stirring, until very tender, 10 to 15 minutes. Add the drained beans, basil, oregano, and thyme and cook over low heat, stirring, until the beans are heated through, 5 to 10 minutes. Set aside to cool.

4. Transfer the bean mixture to a food processor fitted with the metal blade. Add the sour cream and pulse until smooth. Add the lemon juice and season with salt and pepper to taste. Pulse until smooth. Serve warm.

• *Nutritional content per serving: 8 servings per recipe: Cals.: 245; % of cals. from fat: 15; Fat: 4g; Sat. fat: 1g; Carbs: 40g; Fiber: 10g; Sugars: 6g; Cholesterol: 1mg; Protein: 14g; Sodium: 417mg*

# wild rice & toasted almonds

Nutty and aromatic wild rice goes well with all types of meat, poultry, and fish dishes. Even though the general rule of thumb when cooking wild rice is 3 parts liquid to 1 part rice, cooking times and ratios can vary, so it is best to read package directions carefully when cooking wild rice or wild rice blend.

**SERVES 6**

1 CUP WILD RICE, RINSED AND DRAINED
2 CUPS WATER
1 CUP 99% FAT-FREE CHICKEN BROTH
1 TABLESPOON OLIVE OIL
⅓ CUP CHOPPED ALMONDS, LIGHTLY TOASTED (SEE NOTE)
KOSHER SALT AND FRESHLY GROUND BLACK PEPPER

1. Put the rice, water, broth, and butter or olive oil in a saucepan with a tight-fitting lid. Bring to a boil, reduce the heat, cover and simmer for 45 minutes; do not remove the lid. Remove from the heat and let sit for 10 minutes.

2. Before serving, fluff the rice with a fork, stir in the almonds, and toss well. Season with salt and pepper to taste and serve at once.

continued

**Note:** To toast the almonds, spread them on a baking sheet and toast them in a preheated oven or toaster oven for about 3 to 5 minutes or until golden brown and fragrant. Shake the pan once or twice for even toasting. Slide the nuts off the baking sheet as soon as they reach the desired color to halt the cooking. Let cool.

• *Nutritional content per serving: 6 servings per recipe: Cals.: 137; % of cals. from fat: 28; Fat: 4g; Sat. fat: trace; Carbs: 21g; Fiber: 2g; Sugars: 1g; Cholesterol: 0mg; Protein: 5g; Sodium: 360mg*

# herbed couscous

Couscous is a form of semolina that is a staple of North African and Middle Eastern cooking. Although it is sold in boxes, it is best when purchased in bulk from a Middle Eastern market or health food store.

**SERVES 6**

1½ CUPS COUSCOUS
1 CUP 99% FAT-FREE CHICKEN OR VEGETABLE BROTH
1 CUP WATER
1 TABLESPOON PLUS 1 TEASPOON EXTRA-VIRGIN OLIVE OIL
¼ CUP CHOPPED FRESH MINT
½ CUP CHOPPED FRESH FLAT-LEAF PARSLEY
1 TO 2 TABLESPOONS FRESH LEMON JUICE

1. Put the couscous in a large bowl. Put the broth, water, and 1 tablespoon of the olive oil in a small saucepan and bring to a boil. Pour over the couscous and stir well. Cover the bowl with plastic wrap and let the couscous steep until all of the broth mixture is absorbed, about 10 minutes.

2. Fluff the couscous with a fork. Add the mint, parsley, lemon juice, and 1 teaspoon of olive oil and mix well to combine. Taste and adjust the seasonings and stir again. Serve warm or at room temperature.

• *Nutritional content per serving: 6 servings per recipe: Cals.: 197; % of cals. from fat: 18; Fat: 4g; Sat. fat: trace; Carbs: 35g; Fiber: trace; Sugars: trace; Cholesterol: 0mg; Protein: 7g; Sodium: 197mg*

## GOING WITH THE GRAIN

Whole grains of all kinds are packed with nutritious flavor. While we tend to stick with refined grains, it is important to increase our intake of whole wheat, brown rice, and other grains that still retain their nutrients and fiber. Look for these less familiar varieties:

**Teff:** This is the world's smallest grain. Since it's too tiny to process, it isn't stripped of nutrients like refined grains. As a result, it's rich in protein and calcium, and it's gluten-free. It has a sweet, nutty flavor and is sometimes eaten as a hot breakfast cereal. It comes in different colors.

**Quinoa:** Cooks quickly, has a mild flavor, and a slightly crunchy texture. It has a lot of the amino acid lysine, so it provides a more complete protein than many other cereal grains. It comes in different colors, ranging from a pale yellow to red to black. Rinse quinoa before using to remove its bitter natural coating. Substitutes: couscous, rice, bulgur, millet, buckwheat groats, amaranth.

**Amaranth:** These tiny ancient seeds have been cultivated in the Americas for several millennia. They're rich in protein and calcium, and have a pleasant, peppery flavor. Substitutes: millet, quinoa, buckwheat groats.

**Millet:** Unhulled millet is widely used as birdseed, but many health food stores carry hulled millet for human consumption. It's nutritious and gluten-free, and has a very mild flavor that can be improved by toasting the grains. Substitutes: quinoa, bulgur, couscous.

# eat your vegetables

Vegetables bring an exciting array of shapes, flavors and textures to any meal and they are packed with fiber and nutrients that are vital to good health. Their nutritional gifts include the fact that they are all naturally low in calories, help in the fight against heart disease and their high fiber contents helps delay the absorption of glucose. A diet high in vegetables has also been associated with a reduce risk of developing type 2 diabetes. Aim for a minimum of three servings a day—each serving is the equivalent of 1 cup of leafy vegetables (raw), ½ cup of raw or cooked vegetables, such as carrots or green beans, or ½ cup of vegetable juice. Although many vegetables are starchy, non-starchy vegetables such as spinach, broccoli, lettuce, greens, carrots, chilies, peppers and tomatoes contain a small amount of carbohydrate—5 grams per serving. Standard vegetables such as tomatoes and broccoli, spinach and beans are packed with goodness. But if you are interested in making your vegetables a bit more exciting try exotic types that are listed here.

BOK CHOY   This Chinese cabbage has a light, sweet flavor and is good in stir frys and soups. It's high in vitamins A and C and calcium.

CHAYOTE SQUASH   Also called the vegetable pear, this gourd-like squash has a pale green skin. You can bake, steam, or stuff it. It was a mainstay of the Aztec diet.

CELERY ROOT   This brown, gnarly plant, the shape and size of a softball, can be eaten raw or cooked as a salad or a side dish. It is loaded with vitamin C, potassium, and phosphorous.

FENNEL   Offering a good percent of your vitamin C and fiber requirements, licorice-tasting fennel is delicious served raw in salads or braised and roasted as a side dish.

JERUSALEM ARTICHOKE   This is not really an artichoke, but the tuber of the sunflower. Eaten raw or cooked they contain a good supply of iron.

KOHLRABI   A member of the cabbage family, not a root vegetable, these turnip like plants are served mashed, stewed or roasted; the greens can also be eaten. One serving has 140% of your recommended daily dose of vitamin C and almost a fifth of your needed fiber.

RUTABAGA   This comes in white, purple or yellow with a white or yellow flesh and is used in stews and casseroles. High in sugar, it is also loaded with vitamins A and C, calcium, and fiber.

chapter seven **desserts & drinks**

E very party demands at least one dynamite dessert. These special treats can include calorie-sparing Orange Angel Food Cake with Fresh Strawberry Rhubarb Sauce, deceptively light Yogurt, Blueberry, & Toasted Walnut Parfaits, or Chilled Minted Fruit as well as richer-tasting Chocolate-Hazelnut Fondue with Fresh Fruit. The secret of enjoying these is desserts is to eat small portions and make them a once-in-a-while special event.

# lemon–poppy seed cake

This is a moist, tender, and delicious cake that has a fraction of the fat in it, thanks to the buttermilk and oil.

**SERVES 12**

1 TABLESPOON PLUS 1¼ CUPS SUGAR

2 CUPS UNBLEACHED ALL-PURPOSE FLOUR

3 TABLESPOONS POPPY SEEDS

2 TEASPOONS BAKING POWDER

1 TEASPOON BAKING SODA

½ TEASPOON SALT

1 LARGE EGG

1 CUP BUTTERMILK

3 TABLESPOONS CANOLA OIL

1 TABLESPOON FRESH LEMON JUICE

2 TEASPOONS FRESHLY GRATED LEMON ZEST

1 TEASPOON PURE VANILLA EXTRACT

**1.**  Preheat the oven to 350°F. Lightly oil a 6- or 8-cup tube pan. Sprinkle the pan with 1 tablespoon sugar, tapping out the excess.

**2.**  In a large bowl, whisk together the flour, poppy seeds, baking powder, baking soda, and salt.

**3.**  In another bowl, whisk the egg until frothy. Whisk in the 1¼ cups of sugar, buttermilk, oil, lemon juice, lemon zest, and vanilla. Gradually add the wet ingredients to the dry ingredients, whisking until just moistened. Pour the batter into the prepared pan.

**4.**  Bake the cake for 30 to 40 minutes, or until a cake tester inserted in the center comes out clean. Loosen the edges and invert onto a wire rack. Let cool completely.

• *Nutritional content per serving: 12 servings per recipe: Cals.: 214; % of cals. from fat: 22; Fat: 5g; Sat. fat: trace; Carbs: 39g; Fiber: 1g; Sugars: 23g; Cholesterol: 18mg; Protein: 4g; Sodium: 186mg*

# orange angel food cake with fresh strawberry rhubarb sauce

Light and airy angel food cake is a perfect summertime dessert, and when flavored with a little orange zest, its appeal is heightened. With the addition of Strawberry Rhubarb Sauce and a scoop of vanilla sorbet or frozen yogurt, you turn this simple cake into an elaborate dessert.

**SERVES 10**

1½ CUPS SUPERFINE SUGAR

1 CUP UNBLEACHED ALL-PURPOSE FLOUR

½ TEASPOON SALT

12 LARGE EGG WHITES, AT ROOM TEMPERATURE

1 TEASPOON CREAM OF TARTAR

1½ TEASPOONS PURE VANILLA EXTRACT

ZEST OF 1 SMALL ORANGE, FINELY GRATED

**STRAWBERRY RHUBARB SAUCE:**

2 CUPS FINELY DICED FRESH RHUBARB (ABOUT 3 STALKS)

1 PINT STRAWBERRIES, HULLED AND HALVED

⅓ CUP WATER

⅓ CUP SUGAR

VANILLA SORBET OR FROZEN YOGURT, FOR SERVING (OPTIONAL)

1. Preheat the oven to 325°F.

2. In a small bowl, whisk together ½ cup of the superfine sugar with the flour and salt.

3. In a clean, dry bowl of an electric mixer fitted with a clean, dry wire whip or beaters, beat the egg whites until they are foamy. Sprinkle with cream of tartar and beat until soft peaks form. Beat in the vanilla and orange zest and the remaining 1 cup of superfine sugar, a tablespoon at a time, and continue beating until the peaks are stiff, but not dry. Using a rubber spatula, fold the flour mixture into the batter. Do not overmix.

4. Scrape the batter into an ungreased 10-inch tube pan or angel food cake pan. Bake for 50 to 55 minutes, until the cake springs back when lightly touched.

*continued*

5. Place a wine or any long, thin-necked bottle on the counter. Remove the cake from the oven. Turn the pan upside down and place it over the wine bottle so the neck of the bottle is inside the center tube of the pan. Allow the cake to sit like this until it is completely cooled. When completely cool, run a kitchen knife around the side of the pan to loosen. Invert the cake onto a platter.

6. While the cake is cooling, put the rhubarb, strawberries, water, and sugar in a medium nonreactive saucepan. Bring to a boil over high heat, stirring. Lower the heat and simmer, uncovered, stirring occasionally, until the mixture thickens, 20 to 30 minutes.

7. Serve the cake with the warm sauce and a scoop of vanilla sorbet or frozen yogurt, if desired.

*• Nutritional content per serving: 10 servings per recipe: Cals.: 219; % of cals. from fat: 1; Fat: trace; Sat. fat: 0; Carbs: 49g; Fiber: 2g; Sugars: 38g; Cholesterol: 0mg; Protein: 6g; Sodium: 184mg*

## THE HEALTH CONNECTION

Sugar and sweeteners are not the bad guys that they once were thought to be if—and only if—they are figured into overall carbohydrate and calorie consumption, not added to it. And premeal insulin dosing or other glucose-lowering medications are adjusted suitably as needed. The American Diabetes Association says that current research shows that eating sugar (sucrose) doesn't increase blood sugar levels any more than equivalent amounts of other carbohydrates and "does not need to be restricted because of concern about aggravating hyperglycemia [high blood sugar]." In addition they state that "there is no reason to recommend that people with diabetes avoid naturally occurring fructose in fruits, vegetables, and other foods." We have not chosen to use any sugar substitutes in the recipes in this cookbook, feeling that the consumption of natural sugars combined with responsible diabetes management is the best health option and that naturally occurring sugars produce the best results in the recipes themselves.

# chocolate chip cake

Here is a delicious cake that is good to make for a big party. Because it is made with buttermilk and oil, it will remain very moist.

**SERVES 16**

4 LARGE EGG WHITES
¼ TEASPOON CREAM OF TARTAR
1½ CUPS SUGAR
2½ CUPS UNBLEACHED ALL-PURPOSE FLOUR
2 TEASPOONS BAKING POWDER
1½ TEASPOON BAKING SODA
1 TEASPOON SALT
1½ CUPS BUTTERMILK
¼ CUP CANOLA OIL
1 TABLESPOON PURE VANILLA EXTRACT
½ CUP MINI DARK CHOCOLATE CHIPS

**CHOCOLATE ICING:**
⅓ CUP MINI DARK CHOCOLATE CHIPS
2 TABLESPOONS 1% LOW-FAT MILK

1.  Preheat the oven to 350°F. Lightly oil a 12-cup Bundt pan.
2.  In a large bowl, beat the egg whites with an electric mixer on low speed until foamy. Add the cream of tartar, increase the speed to medium-high and beat until soft peaks form. Gradually add ½ cup of the sugar, beating until stiff, but not dry, about 5 minutes.
3.  In another large bowl, combine the remaining 1 cup of sugar, flour, baking powder, baking soda, and salt. With the mixer on medium speed, beat in the buttermilk, oil, vanilla, and a heaping spoonful of egg whites. Using a whisk, fold in the remaining whites and ½ cup chocolate chips. Scrape the batter into the prepared pan, smoothing the top.
4.  Bake the cake for 40 to 50 minutes, or until a cake tester inserted in the center comes out clean. Let cool in the pan on a wire rack for 10 minutes. Invert onto the rack and let cool completely.

*continued*

**5.** To make the icing, combine the ⅓ cup chocolate chips and milk in a saucepan. Heat over very low heat, stirring, until the chocolate is melted and the mixture is smooth. Drizzle over the cake and let stand for about 35 minutes before slicing.

> • *Nutritional content per serving: 16 servings per recipe: Cals.: 269; % of cals. from fat: 30; Fat: 9g; Sat. fat: 3g; Carbs: 45g; Fiber: 2g; Sugars: 29g; Cholesterol: 1mg; Protein: 4g; Sodium: 350mg*

# gingerbread-spice cake

This delicious dark and spicy cake is flavored with blackstrap molasses and strong coffee. It's lovely to serve with tea in the afternoon.

**SERVES 8**

2 CUPS UNBLEACHED ALL-PURPOSE FLOUR
½ CUP SUGAR
1½ TEASPOONS GROUND CINNAMON
1½ TEASPOONS GROUND GINGER
½ TEASPOON SALT
¼ CUP FINELY CHOPPED CRYSTALLIZED GINGER
1½ TEASPOONS BAKING SODA
⅔ CUP STRONG BLACK COFFEE
1 CUP BLACKSTRAP MOLASSES
1 LARGE EGG WHITE
1 TABLESPOON CANOLA OIL
CONFECTIONERS' SUGAR, FOR DUSTING

**1.** Preheat the oven to 350°F. Lightly oil an 8-inch square baking pan. Line the bottom of the pan with a square of parchment or waxed paper and lightly oil it.

**2.** In a large bowl, sift together the flour, sugar, cinnamon, ground ginger, and salt. Add the crystallized ginger and stir to coat.

**3.** In another bowl, stir the baking soda into the coffee. Whisk in the molasses, egg white, and oil. Slowly add into the dry ingredients and stir until just blended. Do not overmix or the cake will be tough.

**4.** Scrape the batter into the prepared pan and bake for 30 to 40 minutes, or until a cake tester inserted in the center comes out clean. Cool in the pan on a rack for 5 minutes. Turn the cake out onto a wire rack and let cool to lukewarm.

**5.** Sprinkle the cake with confectioners' sugar and serve.

• *Nutritional content per serving: 8 servings per recipe: Cals. 284; % of cals. from fat: 6; Fat: 2g; Sat. fat: trace; Carbs: 64g; Fiber: 1g; Sugars: 37g; Cholesterol: 0mg; Protein: 4g; Sodium: 404mg*

# strawberry-rhubarb tart

Fresh, sweet strawberries and tart rhubarb are an unbeatable combination, and they taste fantastic together in this dessert.

**SERVES 8**

**FILLING:**

2 CUPS DICED FRESH RHUBARB

3 CUPS FRESH STRAWBERRIES, HULLED AND THINLY SLICED

¼ CUP SUGAR

½ TEASPOON FRESHLY GRATED LEMON ZEST

1 TABLESPOON CORNSTARCH

1 TABLESPOON COLD WATER

**PIECRUST:**

½ CUP ROLLED OATS

3 TABLESPOONS 1% LOW-FAT MILK

½ TEASPOON PURE VANILLA EXTRACT

⅔ CUP UNBLEACHED ALL-PURPOSE FLOUR

¼ CUP SUGAR

1 TEASPOON FRESHLY GRATED LEMON ZEST

¾ TEASPOON BAKING POWDER

¼ TEASPOON SALT

2 TABLESPOONS CANOLA OIL

3 TABLESPOONS RED CURRANT JELLY

continued

1. To make the filling, in a large nonreactive saucepan, combine the rhubarb, 1 cup of the strawberries, sugar, and ½ teaspoon lemon zest. Let the mixture sit for 20 minutes. Bring to a simmer over medium-low heat and cook, stirring often, until the rhubarb is tender, but still holds its shape, 5 to 8 minutes.

2. Meanwhile, in a small bowl, stir the cornstarch and water until smooth. Stir into the simmering fruit. Cook, stirring constantly, until the mixture is clear and very thick, about 1 minute. Transfer the mixture to a bowl. Cover with a piece of plastic wrap directly on the surface and refrigerate until chilled, about 1 hour. The filling will keep, covered, in the refrigerator, for up to 2 days.

3. To make the crust, preheat the oven to 350°F. Lightly oil a 9-inch tart pan with a removable bottom.

4. Spread the oats on a baking sheet and bake, stirring occasionally, until toasted, 8 to 10 minutes. Let cool. Transfer the oats to a food processor and process until finely ground.

5. In a small bowl, combine the milk and vanilla. In a large bowl, whisk together the ground oats, flour, sugar, 1 teaspoon lemon zest, baking powder, and salt. Drizzle the oil into the dry ingredients and stir with a fork or your fingers until crumbly. Use a fork to stir in the milk mixture, 1 tablespoon at a time, until the dough just comes together.

6. Turn the dough out onto a floured work surface and knead about 8 times. Roll the dough out into an 11-inch circle, dusting with flour, if necessary. Transfer to the prepared pan, pressing to fit. Trim the edges.

7. Line the tart shell with a piece of foil and fill with pie weights or dried beans. Bake the tart shell for 10 to 12 minutes, or until set. Remove the weights or beans and bake for 8 to 12 minutes more, or until lightly browned. Cool in the pan on a wire rack. The shell will keep, loosely covered with foil, for up to 1 day.

8. Shortly before serving, spread the reserved strawberry-rhubarb filling evenly into the tart shell. Arrange the remaining 2 cups of strawberries over the filling.

9. In a small saucepan, heat the jelly over low heat, stirring constantly. With a pastry brush, glaze the strawberries with the jelly.

• *Nutritional content per serving: 8 servings per recipe: Cals.: 185; % of cals. from fat: 20; Fat: 4g; Sat. fat: trace; Carbs: 36g; Fiber: 3g; Sugars: 20g; Cholesterol: 0mg; Protein: 3g; Sodium: 115mg*

# lemon cookies

Luscious lemon cookies are good to serve with sorbet or frozen yogurt for a light dessert. They're also great to make ahead of time since they will keep for up to 3 days in an airtight container; and they can also be frozen.

**MAKES ABOUT 2 DOZEN COOKIES**

2½ CUPS PASTRY FLOUR
1 TEASPOON BAKING POWDER
1 TEASPOON BAKING SODA
½ TEASPOON SALT
1¼ CUPS SUGAR
½ CUP UNSWEETENED APPLESAUCE
¼ CUP CANOLA OIL
2 TABLESPOONS FRESH LEMON JUICE
1 TABLESPOON FRESHLY GRATED LEMON ZEST

1. In a large bowl, whisk together the flour, baking powder, baking soda, and salt.

2. In another large bowl, whisk together 1 cup of the sugar, the applesauce, oil, lemon juice, and lemon zest until smooth. Make a well in the dry ingredients and add the wet ingredients. Stir until blended. Cover the dough with plastic wrap and refrigerate until chilled, about 1 hour. The dough will keep in the refrigerator for up to 3 days.

3. Preheat the oven to 350°F. Lightly oil 2 baking sheets.

4. Put the remaining ¼ cup of sugar in a small bowl. Using floured hands, roll the dough into 1½-inch balls. Roll the balls in the sugar to coat and place on the baking sheets 2 inches apart.

5. Bake the cookies until very lightly browned, 12 to 14 minutes. Cool on the baking sheet for 1 minute, then transfer to a wire rack to cool completely. The cookies will keep in an airtight container for up to 3 days and can be frozen for up to 1 month.

• *Nutritional content per serving: 2 cookies per serving: Cals.: 216; % of cals. from fat: 21; Fat: 5g; Sat. fat: trace; Carbs: 41g; Fiber: 4g; Sugars: 21g; Cholesterol: 0mg; Protein: 3g; Sodium: 233mg*

# oatmeal raisin cookies

In baking, toasted oats give cookies and piecrusts a deliciously nutty flavor. This recipe makes a generous amount of cookies, which is great for times when you have a houseful of hungry kids (or adults).

**MAKES ABOUT 5 DOZEN COOKIES**

3 CUPS ROLLED OATS
2 CUPS UNBLEACHED ALL-PURPOSE FLOUR
1 TEASPOON GROUND CINNAMON
½ TEASPOON BAKING POWDER
1 TEASPOON BAKING SODA
½ TEASPOON SALT
1 CUP SUGAR
½ CUP LIGHT BROWN SUGAR
½ CUP UNSWEETENED APPLESAUCE
2 LARGE EGGS, AT ROOM TEMPERATURE
¼ CUP CANOLA OIL
1 CUP RAISINS

1. Preheat the oven to 375°F. Lightly oil 2 baking sheets.
2. Spread the oats on another baking sheet and bake, stirring occasionally, until toasted, 8 to 10 minutes. Let cool.
3. In a small bowl, whisk together the flour, cinnamon, baking powder, baking soda, and salt. Set aside.
4. In a large bowl, beat the sugars, applesauce, eggs, and oil, using an electric mixer, until fluffy. Blend in the dry flour mixture by hand. Stir in the oats and raisins until well blended.
5. Drop the dough by rounded teaspoons, 1½ inches apart, onto the prepared baking sheets. Bake until lightly browned, 10 to 12 minutes. Transfer the cookies to a rack to cool completely. The cookies will keep in an airtight container for up to 2 days and can be frozen for up to 1 month.

• *Nutritional content per serving: 2 cookies per serving: Cals.: 128; % of cals. from fat: 21; Fat: 3g; Sat. fat: trace; Carbs: 23g; Fiber: 2g; Sugars: 14g; Cholesterol: 14g; Protein: 3g; Sodium: 94mg*

# creamy lemon-rice pudding

Your guests will love this simple and wonderful comfort food dessert, creamy rice pudding scented with lemon zest and cinnamon sticks.

**SERVES 8**

6 CUPS 1% LOW-FAT MILK
1 CUP ARBORIO RICE
½ CUP SUGAR
TWO 4-INCH STRIPS LEMON ZEST
2 CINNAMON STICKS
½ TEASPOON SALT
1 TEASPOON PURE VANILLA EXTRACT
GROUND CINNAMON, FOR GARNISH

1.  In a heavy large saucepan, combine the milk, rice, sugar, lemon zest, cinnamon sticks, and salt. Bring to a simmer over low heat and cook, stirring occasionally, until the rice is tender and creamy, about 20 minutes. Remove from the heat. Remove the lemon zest and cinnamon sticks. Stir in the vanilla. Cover and let rest for 10 minutes.

2.  Serve the pudding warm, dusted with cinnamon.

• *Nutritional content per serving: 8 servings per recipe: Cals.: 200; % of cals. from fat: 9; Fat: 2g; Sat. fat: 1g; Carbs: 38g; Fiber: trace; Sugars: 21g; Cholesterol: 9g; Protein: 8g; Sodium: 237mg*

## THE HEALTH CONNECTION

Arborio rice is a pearly, small-grained Italian white rice used for risotto. Its starch is released during cooking, making it much creamier than other rice. Every 100 grams (about ¼ cup) of white rice has 82 grams of carbs, jasmine or Thai rice has 81 grams of carbs, brown rice has 77 grams of carbs, and glutenous rice has 81 grams of carbs. That may be more than half your targeted intake of carbs in a day, so plan accordingly.

# ginger & pumpkin flans

These utterly delicious flans are a nice change from holiday pumpkin pie. They are quite easy to make and can be prepared a few days ahead of time.

**SERVES 6**

¾ CUP PLUS ⅓ CUP SUGAR
⅓ CUP WATER
2 LARGE EGGS, AT ROOM TEMPERATURE
4 LARGE EGG WHITES, AT ROOM TEMPERATURE
1 CUP CANNED PUMPKIN PUREE
1 TEASPOON GRATED FRESH GINGER
1 TEASPOON PURE VANILLA EXTRACT
¾ CUP 1% LOW-FAT MILK
¾ CUP EVAPORATED SKIM MILK

1. Preheat the oven to 325°F.

2. In a small heavy saucepan, combine ¾ cup sugar with the water. Bring to a simmer over low heat, stirring occasionally, until the sugar melts. Increase the heat to medium-high and cook until the caramel turns amber, 5 to 7 minutes. Do not let it burn. Carefully pour the caramel into six ¾-cup ramekins and tilt to coat the inside of each ramekin thoroughly. Set aside.

3. In a mixing bowl, whisk the eggs, egg whites, and remaining ⅓ cup sugar until smooth. Add the pumpkin puree, ginger, and vanilla, and whisk again until smooth. Add the milks and gently stir until well incorporated. Pour the mixture into the prepared ramekins.

4. Put the ramekins in a roasting pan. Add a enough boiling water to the pan to come halfway up the outsides of the ramekins.

5. Bake the flans for 45 to 50 minutes, or until a knife inserted in their centers comes out clean. Remove ramekins from the bath and let cool on a wire rack. Cover and refrigerate until chilled, at least 2 hours. The flans will keep, covered, in the refrigerator for up to 2 days.

6. To serve, run a sharp knife around the edge of each flan and invert onto dessert bowls or plates.

• *Nutritional content per serving: 6 servings per recipe: Cals.: 223; % of cals. from fat: 8; Fat: 2g; Sat. fat: 1g; Carbs: 44g; Fiber: 1g; Sugars: 41g; Cholesterol: 72mg; Protein: 8g; Sodium: 117mg*

## HOLIDAY FEASTING

With all the wonderful recipes in this book, it may seem daunting to imagine that you can make it through the holidays without adding a few pounds or throwing your nutritional plan and glucose levels out of whack. But while it's true that holidays can be a challenge for those trying to avoid extra calories and fat, a healthy holiday season doesn't mean that you have to eliminate your favorite foods.

When faced with your all-time favorites, such as stuffing or baked yams or pumpkin pie, eat just a small taste. Making small reductions in the amount you eat will save a lot of calories: Eating only about half a muffin cuts 150 calories; passing on a ½ cup of rice eliminates 200 calories, skipping the mayo on a turkey sandwich (use mustard) shaves around 100 to 200 calories.

Another smart move: don't go to a party or dinner hungry. Have a snack beforehand so you can eat more moderately. You can also fill up on so-called "free foods"; that is those that don't figure into your daily intake of calories and carbs. They include bouillon, sugar-free carbonated beverages, unsweetened cranberries and rhubarb, cabbage, celery, cucumber, mushrooms, salad greens, and sugar-free candy, gelatin, gum, jam, or syrup. Also included as free foods are condiments such as catsup, horseradish and mustard, and many salsas.

You can also use substitutes for some ingredients in holiday dishes without losing flavor or appeal.
- Nonstick cookware or cooking sprays can be used to reduce fat needed for cooking.
- Unsweetened applesauce can be used in baking cookies. Replace half of the butter called for with applesauce.
- Reduce the number of eggs in a recipe by using two egg whites for one whole egg; in recipes that call for 3 or more eggs, use one whole egg and two egg whites for each additional egg.
- Avoid solid vegetable shortenings to eliminate trans fats.
- Replace sour cream with nonfat yogurt or fat-free sour cream.
- Opt for 1% milk in place of whole or 2% milk.
- Use lowfat ricotta cheese in place of cream in some recipes. Blend it to make it smooth.
- Use lowfat cheese when possible in sauces and casseroles—add just before serving; it doesn't perform well with high or direct heat. Nonfat cheese does not cook well.
- Choose beverages wisely—sugary and alcoholic drinks can pile on hidden calories and carbohydrates.

# Thanksgiving

Crostini with Roasted Eggplant Spread
(page 24)

Pickled Party Shrimp
(page 6)

Carrot & Ginger Soup
(page 42)

Endive, Beet & Walnut Salad
(page 64)

Holiday Roast Turkey
with Rice & Spinach Stuffing
(page 122)

Roasted Root Vegetables
(page 182)

Braised Pearl Onions, Shallots, & Leeks
(page 179)

Ginger & Pumpkin Flans
(page 210)

Poached Pears in Beaujolais
(page 221)

# yogurt, blueberry, & toasted walnut parfaits

Who knew that something so yummy could be so good for you? These refreshing parfaits are made with yogurt, blueberries, and walnuts, all superfoods that are packed with potassium and protein as well as a variety of vitamins. Although it is not absolutely necessary to drain the yogurt in this recipe, the process makes it creamier and less watery.

**SERVES 6**

6 CUPS PLAIN LOW-FAT YOGURT
2 CUPS WALNUT HALVES
4 CUPS FRESH BLUEBERRIES
2 TABLESPOONS SUGAR
½ TEASPOON GROUND CINNAMON

1. Line a large sieve with cheesecloth and place it over a large bowl. Put the yogurt in the sieve and let it drain for 10 to 15 minutes. Transfer the yogurt from the sieve to a medium bowl. This may have to be done in batches. Put the yogurt in the refrigerator for at least 1 hour and up to 6 hours.

2. Preheat the oven to 350°F. Put the walnuts on a baking sheet and bake, shaking the pan occasionally, until lightly toasted, 5 to 7 minutes. Be very careful not to burn the walnuts.

3. Put the blueberries in a large bowl. In a small bowl, mix together the sugar and cinnamon, add to the blueberries and stir to mix well.

4. To assemble the parfaits, spoon the yogurt to coat the bottom of each glass (see Note). Top with a layer of blueberries and walnuts. Repeat with another layer of yogurt, blueberries, and walnuts. Refrigerate the parfaits until ready to serve.

**Note:** The parfaits can be assembled in parfait glasses, wine glasses, or tumblers.

• *Nutritional content per serving: 6 servings per recipe: Cals.: 490; % of cals. from fat: 55; Fat: 30g; Sat. fat: 5g; Carbs: 44g; Fiber: 5g; Sugars: 27g; Cholesterol: 14mg; Protein: 20g; Sodium: 208mg*

# grilled bananas & pineapple

For a quick, easy, and delicious dessert, try grilling fresh fruit. This combination of grilled fresh pineapple and bananas is very good. Other good fruits for grilling are peaches, plums, nectarines, and mangoes.

**SERVES 6**

6 FRESH PINEAPPLE RINGS, ABOUT ½ INCH THICK
3 BANANAS, UNPEELED, CUT IN HALF LENGTHWISE
FRESH LIME JUICE
LIME WEDGES, FOR GARNISH

1.  Prepare a gas or charcoal grill. When the fire is medium-hot, and the coals are covered with a light coating of ash and glow deep red, put the pineapple rings on the grill and cook, turning occasionally, until lightly browned, about 8 to 10 minutes. Put the bananas on the grill, cut side down, until lightly browned, about 4 to 6 minutes. Remove from the heat and transfer to a platter.

2.  Sprinkle the pineapple rings and bananas generously with fresh lime juice. Put a pineapple ring and banana half on dessert plates, garnish with lime wedges, and serve.

• *Nutritional content per serving: 6 servings per recipe: Cals.: 133; % of cals. from fat: 0; Fat: 0g; Sat. fat: trace; Carbs: 35g; Fiber: 4g; Sugars: 18g; Cholesterol: 9mg; Protein: 1g; Sodium: 2mg*

# grilled peaches
# with red wine sauce

Fresh peaches are good to cook on the grill after the fire has died down a bit. They don't require a lot of time or attention, just a bit of basting with a sauce of red wine and brown sugar. They're delicious hot off the grill with a scoop of vanilla sorbet.

**SERVES 8**

4 LARGE RIPE PEACHES, PITTED AND HALVED
CORN OIL, FOR BRUSHING
2 CUPS FRUITY RED WINE, SUCH AS ZINFANDEL
   OR BEAUJOLAIS NOUVEAU
2 TABLESPOONS BROWN SUGAR
VANILLA SORBET, FOR SERVING

1. Prepare a gas or charcoal grill. Brush the peaches with corn oil. Whisk the wine and sugar together until well combined.

2. When the fire is medium-hot, and the coals are covered with a light coating of ash and glow deep red, place the peaches on the grill, cut side down, cook about 3 minutes, and turn. Brush with the red wine mixture and continue cooking until fork-tender, for 20 to 25 minutes, turning and basting often.

3. To serve, spoon a bit of the wine sauce into a shallow bowl, add the grilled peach, drizzle with a bit more sauce and serve with a scoop of sorbet.

• *Nutritional content per serving: 8 servings per recipe: Cals.: 91; % of cals. from fat: 8; Fat: 1g; Sat. fat: trace; Carbs: 12g; Fiber: 1g; Sugars: 11g; Cholesterol: 0mg; Protein: 1g; Sodium: 4mg*

# chocolate-hazelnut fondue with fresh fruit

For a festive fondue dessert, dip pieces of fruit, such as strawberries, kiwi, and bananas, and cubes of angel food cake into Chocolate-Hazelnut Sauce.

**SERVES 6 TO 8**

**CHOCOLATE-HAZELNUT SAUCE:**
⅔ CUP FAT-FREE CHOCOLATE SYRUP
¼ CUP CHOCOLATE HAZELNUT SPREAD, SUCH AS NUTELLA®

1 PINT FRESH STRAWBERRIES, RINSED
3 KIWIS, PEELED, HALVED, AND CUT INTO ½-INCH-THICK SLICES
2 BANANAS, PEELED AND CUT INTO ½-INCH ROUNDS
HALF OF A 10-INCH ANGEL FOOD CAKE, CUT INTO 1-INCH CUBES

1. To make the sauce, in a small saucepan, stir the chocolate syrup and chocolate hazelnut spread together over low heat until smooth and warm. The sauce will keep, covered, in the refrigerator for up to 1 week.

2. You may warm the Chocolate-Hazelnut Sauce, if desired, or serve it at room temperature. Place a small bowl of the Chocolate-Hazelnut Sauce in the center of a large platter. Arrange the fruit and cake around the sauce. Serve with long toothpicks or fondue forks.

**Note:** Other fruits can be used, such as peeled and sectioned seedless oranges, mangoes, papayas, star fruit, and cherries.

• *Nutritional content per serving: 6 to 8 servings per recipe: Cals.: 272; % of cals. from fat: 9; Fat: 3g; Sat. fat: trace; Carbs: 59g; Fiber: 14g; Sugars: 40g; Cholesterol: 0mg; Protein: 5g; Sodium: 93mg*

# Valentine's Day Dinner

Winter Fruit Salad
with Walnuts & Goat Cheese
(page 68)

Roasted Cornish Game Hens
with Citrus Sauce
(page 119)

Red Cabbage & Apple Sauté
(page 175)

Herbed Couscous
(page 192)

Chocolate-Hazelnut Fondue
with Fresh Fruit
(page 218)

❦

# poached pears in beaujolais

Pears are so elegant they are always appropriate for dessert, and this is a simple way to prepare them. They are especially good poached in Beaujolais Nouveau, which arrives in stores in autumn.

**SERVES 6**

6 BOSC PEARS, PEELED WITH STEMS INTACT
¼ CUP SUGAR
4 CUPS FRUITY RED WINE, SUCH AS BEAUJOLAIS NOUVEAU
⅓ CUP CRÈME DE CASSIS
2 TABLESPOONS FRESH LEMON JUICE
1 VANILLA BEAN, SPLIT LENGTHWISE
6 WHOLE CLOVES
FRESH MINT SPRIGS, FOR GARNISH

1. Trim the bottom of the pears so they can sit upright. Put them in a large nonreactive pan.

2. Mix the sugar, wine, crème de cassis, and lemon juice together and pour over the pears. Add the vanilla bean and the cloves.

3. Cover the pan and bring the liquid to a simmer over medium heat. Simmer, partially covered, turning the pears occasionally until they are cooked through and nicely and evenly colored, about 30 minutes.

4. Remove the pan from the heat and let the pears cool in the liquid. Transfer both the pears and the liquid to a glass or ceramic bowl. Cover and refrigerate for 24 hours before serving. Garnish with mint sprigs.

• *Nutritional content per serving: 6 servings per recipe: Cals.: 127; % of cals. from fat: 1; Fat: trace; Sat. fat: 0; Carbs: 30g; Fiber: 5g; Sugars: 20g; Cholesterol: 0mg; Protein: 1g; Sodium: 3mg*

# cider-baked apples

This is a dessert the whole family will love—farm-fresh apples stuffed with dried cranberry raisins and spices, braised in apple cider and honey.

**SERVES 6**

6 LARGE JUICY BAKING APPLES
2 TABLESPOONS LIGHT BROWN SUGAR
½ CUP CHOPPED DRIED CRANBERRY RAISINS
   OR ¼ CUP EACH
1 TEASPOON GROUND CINNAMON
1 TEASPOON FRESHLY GRATED LEMON ZEST
1 CUP APPLE CIDER
1 TABLESPOON HONEY
1 TABLESPOON FRESH LEMON JUICE
1 TABLESPOON UNSALTED BUTTER, CUT INTO 6 PIECES
LOW-FAT VANILLA OR LEMON YOGURT, FOR SERVING (OPTIONAL)

1. Preheat the oven to 375°F. Line a 9 x 13-inch baking dish with foil.
2. Core the apples and arrange in the baking dish.
3. In a small bowl, mix together the sugar, cranberry raisins, cinnamon, and lemon zest. Divide among the apples, spooning it into the cavities.
4. In a small saucepan, heat the cider, honey, and lemon juice over low heat, stirring until the honey melts. Pour the mixture around the apples.
5. Dot each apple with the butter and bake, uncovered. Spoon the pan juices over the apples a few times until they are tender but not mushy when pierced with a knife tip, about 40 minutes.
6. Remove the pan from the oven and continue to spoon the juices over the apples a few times to glaze them as they cool. (The apples can be baked a few hours ahead of time and kept at room temperature. Reheat slightly in the oven before serving.)
7. To serve, spoon the apples and juices onto shallow dessert plates or bowls. Serve slightly warm with a dollop of yogurt, if desired.

• *Nutritional content per serving: 6 servings per recipe: Cals.: 210; % of cals. from fat: 11; Fat: 3g; Sat. fat: 1g; Carbs: 50g; Fiber: 6g; Sugars: 41g; Cholesterol: 5mg; Protein: 1g; Sodium: 1mg*

# Buffet-Style Dinner Party

Assorted Crostini
(page 22–27)

Braised Chicken & Baby Leeks
(page 114)

Roasted Root Vegetables
(page 182)

Sautéed Chickpeas & Swiss Chard
(page 184)

Mixed Green Salad

Lemon–Poppy Seed Cake
(page 199)

Cider-Baked Apples
(page 222)

# honeydew melon & strawberries with lime yogurt sauce

Honeydew melon and strawberries topped with refreshing Lime Yogurt Sauce tastes fantastic and makes a nice light ending to any meal.

**SERVES 8**

1 LARGE RIPE HONEYDEW MELON,
   SEEDED AND CUT INTO 1½-INCH CHUNKS
1 PINT STRAWBERRIES, HULLED AND HALVED
¼ CUP FRESH LIME JUICE
1 TABLESPOON SUGAR

**LIME YOGURT SAUCE:**

2 CUPS PLAIN LOW-FAT YOGURT
¼ CUP SUGAR
1 TABLESPOON FRESHLY GRATED LIME ZEST
1 TABLESPOON FRESH LIME JUICE

1.  In a large bowl, toss the melon, strawberries, lime juice, and sugar together. Let stand for 15 minutes, stirring occasionally.

2.  To make the Lime Yogurt Sauce, in a medium bowl, combine the yogurt, sugar, lime zest, and juice together. Cover and refrigerate until chilled, about 1 hour. The yogurt will keep, covered, in the refrigerator for up to 2 days. Stir well before serving.

3.  Spoon the fruit into bowls and spoon the sauce over each serving. Serve at once.

• *Nutritional content per serving: 8 servings per recipe: Cals.: 73; % of cals. from fat: 10; Fat: 1g; Sat. fat: trace; Carbs: 17g; Fiber: 2g; Sugars: 14g; Cholesterol: 0mg; Protein: 1g; Sodium: 2mg*

# chilled minted fruit

This is one of our favorite ways to serve fruit on a hot day. The cherries, blueberries, and red grapes are a terrific combination. This is a great dessert for a picnic or any casual outdoor get-together.

**SERVES 6**

12 ICE CUBES
1 POUND RIPE CHERRIES, RINSED
1 CUP BLUEBERRIES, RINSED
1 CUP RED GRAPES, RINSED
¾ CUP THINLY SLICED MINT LEAVES

1. Crush the ice in a blender by filling it about three-quarters full of ice cubes. Turn the blender on high and grind up the ice, pulsing the machine on and off if necessary. This may have to be done in 2 batches.

2. Fill a large bowl with the crushed ice, cherries, blueberries, grapes, and mint. Toss together. Refrigerate for at least 1 hour and serve chilled.

• *Nutritional content per serving: 6 servings per recipe: Cals.: 73; % of cals. from fat: 10; Fat: 1g; Sat. fat: trace; Carbs: 17g; Fiber: 2g; Sugars: 14g; Cholesterol: 0mg; Protein: 1g; Sodium: 2mg*

# strawberry-mango coolers

What could be more refreshing than a cooler made with fresh pureed fruit poured over lots of seltzer and ice?

**SERVES 6**

20 STRAWBERRIES, HULLED AND HALVED
1 MANGO, PEELED, PITTED, AND CUT INTO ½-INCH PIECES
6 ICE CUBES
1 QUART SELTZER, OR AS NEEDED
LIME WEDGES, FOR GARNISH

1. Put the strawberries, mango, and ice in a blender and blend until smooth.
2. Pour about 3 tablespoons of the blended fruit into 6 tall glasses. Add seltzer and additional ice to each drink and gently stir to blend. Garnish each drink with a lime wedge and serve.

• *Nutritional content per serving: 6 servings per recipe: Cals.: 39; % of cals. from fat: 7; Fat: trace; Sat. fat: 0; Carbs: 10g; Fiber: 2g; Sugars: 8g; Cholesterol: 0mg; Protein: trace; Sodium: 39mg*

## DRINKS

These festive party drinks are perfect for any gathering and for anyone. There is no alcohol in the recipes. It's true that the American Diabetes Association says that for people with diabetes "the same precautions apply regarding the use of alcohol that apply to the general population." And, "in studies using moderate amounts of alcohol ingested with food in people with type 1 or type 2 diabetes, alcohol had no acute effect on blood glucose or insulin levels." But we feel that the focus here is on food and the extra calories and carbohydrates associated with alcoholic drinks should not be substituted for the delicious foods and beverages presented here. Just our point of view.

# banana-blueberry smoothies

Bananas and blueberries taste great together in this smoothie. It's a good thing to drink after a light meal or as a quick pick-me-up after exercise.

**SERVES 6**

3 RIPE BANANAS, PEELED AND SLICED
2 CUPS LOW-FAT VANILLA YOGURT
2 CUPS FRESH BLUEBERRIES
1 TABLESPOON ORANGE JUICE
6 ICE CUBES

Put the bananas, yogurt, blueberries, orange juice, and ice cubes in a blender. Blend until very smooth. Serve with additional ice, if desired.

• *Nutritional content per serving: 6 servings per recipe: Cals.: 155; % of cals. from fat: 8; Fat: 1g; Sat. fat: 1g; Carbs: 34g; Fiber: 3g; Sugars: 26g; Cholesterol: 5mg; Protein: 4g; Sodium: 58mg*

# minted melon smoothies

Fragrant honeydew melon, rich in vitamin C, is so delicious and so good for you. Try it in this yogurt-based smoothie laced with fresh lime and mint.

**SERVES 6**

1 HONEYDEW MELON, HALVED, SEEDED,
   AND CUT INTO SMALL DICE
2 CUPS LOW-FAT PLAIN YOGURT
1 TEASPOON HONEY
2 TABLESPOONS FRESH LIME JUICE
¼ CUP CHOPPED FRESH MINT
6 ICE CUBES

Put the melon, yogurt, honey, lime juice, mint, and ice cubes in a blender. Blend until very smooth. Serve with additional ice, if desired.

• *Nutritional content per serving: 6 servings per recipe: Cals.: 134; % of cals. from fat: 10; Fat: 2g; Sat. fat: 1g; Carbs: 27g; Fiber: 2g; Sugars: 23g; Cholesterol: 5mg; Protein: 6g; Sodium: 106mg*

# iced mint & lemon verbena tea

This is perfect to drink on a sunny summer afternoon.

**SERVES 6**

2 QUARTS WATER
2 TABLESPOONS MINT TEA LEAVES
8 SPRIGS LEMON VERBENA
LEMON SLICES, FOR GARNISH

1. Bring the water to a full boil in a large saucepan. Add the tea, and remove the pan from the heat. Cover and let stand for 5 minutes. Add the lemon verbena sprigs and let stand for 5 more minutes.

2. Strain into a pitcher and let cool to room temperature. Refrigerate for at least 2 hours. Serve over ice in chilled glasses, garnished with the lemon slices.

# clove-scented orange tea

Fragrant orange-pekoe tea is nicely spiced with whole cloves and orange slices in this lovely recipe.

**SERVES 6**

2 TABLESPOONS ORANGE-PEKOE TEA LEAVES
8 WHOLE CLOVES
2 QUARTS BOILING WATER
3 ORANGE SLICES, HALVED, FOR GARNISH

1. Put the tea leaves and cloves in a large saucepan. Add the boiling water, cover, and let steep for 5 minutes.
2. Stir once and strain the tea mixture into a large teapot or into teacups. Serve the tea garnished with orange slices.

# china-mint tea

Black tea and fresh mint leaves complement each other perfectly in this tasty tea.

**SERVES 6**

2 TABLESPOONS BLACK TEA LEAVES
½ CUP CHOPPED FRESH MINT
2 QUARTS BOILING WATER
LEMON SLICES AND MINT SPRIGS, FOR GARNISH

1. Put the tea leaves and mint in a large saucepan. Add the boiling water, cover, and let steep for 5 minutes.
2. Stir once and strain the tea mixture into a large teapot or into teacups. Serve the tea garnished with lemon slices and mint sprigs.

# iced mocha cinnamon coffee

Here's a warm weather treat to serve to your guests after lunch or dinner.

**SERVES 6**

6 CUPS STRONG HOT BREWED COFFEE
6 OUNCES UNSWEETENED CHOCOLATE
1 CINNAMON STICK
1% LOW-FAT MILK, FOR SERVING

1. Pour the coffee into a large saucepan. Heat the chocolate and cinnamon stick in a double boiler or a pan set over boiling water. Add to the coffee and stir well.

2. Strain into a large pitcher, discarding the cinnamon stick. Let cool to room temperature. Refrigerate for at least 2 hours. Serve over ice in chilled glasses, with milk.

• *Nutritional content per serving: 6 servings per recipe: Cals.: 153; % of cals. from fat: 92; Fat: 116g; Sat. fat: 9g; Carbs: 9g; Fiber: 43g; Sugars: trace; Cholesterol: 0mg; Protein: 3g; Sodium: 9mg*

# rethinking desserts

Sugar used to be forbidden for people with diabetes—now experts understand that within the constraints of a well-designed nutritional plan, sugar is no more disruptive to blood glucose levels than other carbohydrates such as bread or potatoes. As long as you plan for it, you can enjoy sweets and treats. So our attitude is go for the real thing—just make sure it is not too fatty, too calorie intense or too loaded with carbs. Although sugar substitutes have a place in meal planning, the very best approach is to stick with pure, real foods, chosen wisely.

## FINDING A BALANCE

To keep your glucose levels on target, and still enjoy an occasional dessert, make sure you substitute your dessert carbs for planned carbs—keeping your total the same for the meal. For example, if you know you are going to have a piece of pie after dinner, eliminate potatoes from your dinner and drink water instead of juice. If you choose to eat foods that contain sugar substitutes, they do not count as a carbohydrate, a fat, or any other exchange. They are added to your meal plan instead of substituted.

## EATING FRUIT

How fruit affects your blood glucose is highly individual and also depends on whether it is eaten after a fatty meal, on an empty stomach (when glucose levels are already elevated), or whether the fruit is raw or cooked. So check your levels after eating fruit to learn about your individual response and plan accordingly. One portion equals:

- one medium-sized fresh fruit (apple, pear, banana, etc.)
- two small fruits (apricots, plums, kiwi fruit, etc.)
- a cupful of berries or very small fruit (grapes, raspberries, etc.)
- a large slice of a large fruit (melon, pineapple, etc.)
- a small glass of unsweetened fruit juice

## CHOCOLATE

Chocolate, like other sweet treats, has been rehabilitated. Instead of being a forbidden pleasure, it may now have a (small) role in maintaining health. Not only is dark chocolate high in heart-healthy antioxidants, but according to one carefully done study, it helps lower blood pressure and cholesterol and makes it easier for the body to metabolize (burn) sugar. Beware of the extra calories and carbs it packs, and don't add them to your daily totals. But do enjoy.

# index

*Italics* indicate photographs